I ONCE WAS LOST

MARY BROWN

ISBN: 978-1-5356-0924-1

I am dedicating this book to my children:
Floyd, Juan, Gregg, and Lori—the loves of my life.

I heard that God has appointed an angel to watch over all of us.
I truly believe that this is true.
When I look back over my life, I know beyond a shadow of a doubt
that I have an angel watching over my entire family and me!
One day someone asked me the question,
"Mary, do you believe in angels?"
My answer, without wavering, was, "Most definitely!"

Contents

Acknowledgments vii

I once was lost! 1

Summary... 107

About the Author 114

Acknowledgments

I DEDICATE THIS BOOK TO my children Floyd, Juan, Gregg, and Lori. I also want to acknowledge my granddaughter, Tamia, and her son, my great-grandson, Darrell.

From the time of their births to this day, I feel that if I didn't have them in my life, I wouldn't have survived. Because of their existence, I am here today and not a drug addict or lying in my grave. I knew that if I didn't change my way of living, it would have greatly affected my children's lives in a negative way, and I loved them too much to have allowed that to happen—they mean too much to me and I to them. I also want to thank my siblings—those who are still with us and those who have since passed away—for the love that they have shown me through the many years and still show me today. We have always been a close, loving family, and we love family reunions and any gatherings that bring us all together just to be near each other.

I want to thank my good friend, Joyce Cooke, who was kind enough to edit my book and encouraged me to hurry and get it published. She enjoyed reading it and assured me that I would be able to sell it without a doubt. I also knew that she could be trusted to edit it with fairness. I love you, my dear friend! She knows that I am a plain ole country girl and I write the way I talk. I prayed that the Holy Spirit would give me the name of someone whom I could trust to be the first to read the book, and He immediately put Joyce in my mind.

Most of all, I want to give all praise to my Lord and Savior Jesus the Christ. Without Him leading and guiding me throughout my life, I wouldn't be here today. I know with everything that is in me, He ordered my steps all the way through the hurts and pains, through the sunshine and the rain. He promised in His word that He would never leave, nor forsake me, and He never has and He never will. Thank You, dear Lord!

I once was lost!

MANY WOMEN WILL PROBABLY RELATE to my story. However, some may see themselves at the beginning and some at the end. My hope is that my story will let others see that they are not the only ones who have been through rough times but were still able to claim victory because of God's deliverance.

"I come to you for protection, O Lord my God. Save me from my persecutors—rescue me!" (Psalm 7:1).

The Bible tells us that our hope is securely fastened in Jesus Christ who redeemed us once and for all when He died, rose again, and ascended to heaven (Hebrews 6:19). When it comes to our salvation, our hope is anchored in the promise of God and the work of Jesus Christ.

I once was lost!

I still remember Speedy's Wednesday night maninose giveaways. Some called them steamers, we called them maninose.

Every Wednesday night, crowds would gather at Speedy's to eat maninose that Speedy provided for free. Speedy knew that the more maninose that was eaten, the more beer and liquor he would sell, and it was great for everyone concerned. Of course that was a night that would fill the joint up. Folks from miles around would come to that bar/restaurant and have a ball. We would eat, dance, and have a great ole time.

I was there that night dancing with my friend William David. William and I were good friends from elementary school, until we grew up and went our separate ways. William was gay and loved being gay. He had more boyfriends than I had, and we would laugh and talk about it all the time. William and I loved to dance, and we would go to different bars and dance the night away. When I think back to those days, I tell myself that I should have danced all night! When I stopped dancing, that's when I got into trouble.

Riding the bus from school was exciting because cars would follow the bus. When we got off, the cars would stop and guys would get out and walk the rest of the way home with us. This one particular guy would walk and talk with me. After a time, he would put his arms around my shoulders and kiss me on the cheek. I was fourteen years old. Just before we approached the house, they would get back in the car and leave.

I don't mind telling you that I was in love, or so I thought. One day he told me to meet him in the woods because he had a surprise for me. He told me that I would like the surprise. I couldn't wait to get the present he had for me. That particular day, I left from my sister-in-law's house and met him where he told me to.

When I approached him, he was standing by a tree. I asked him where the surprise was. He took my hands and walked me down through the woods. After we were deep in the woods, he pulled me down to the ground and said, "This is the surprise." He pulled up my dress, pulled my panties off, and raped me. I told him to stop because it hurt so badly, but he kept on until he was satisfied. He got up, zipped up his pants, and walked away, leaving me lying there on the ground crying.

I looked down and blood was coming down my legs. I got up and walked to my sister-in-law's house and told her what happened. She helped me to clean up. I don't know when she called my mother, but the next day Mama came and got me and we never spoke of it. That was the end of that relationship. When he would see me, he couldn't look me in the eye, and I felt nothing but hate for him. Sometimes when I go home for funerals, I see him and he still can't look me in the eye. Although he is an old man now, I know that he remembers what he did. Of course I told William about it. He wanted to confront him, but I told him not to.

William knew all my secrets and I knew most of his. We would later lie across my bed and talk about what was happening in our lives. I would tell him about my boyfriend, and he would tell me about his boyfriends. He had many, and they all knew that I knew about them. Most of them were married men. Some were old men, some not so old. When we went out, they would look at me in a strange way, wondering if I knew they were having sex with William. I am getting ahead of myself, so let me go back up a little.

I won't call the rapist by name because I later found out that he was following the bus and starting to walk with my cousin. She was very much in love with him, and after a few years they got married.

> **"I will lift up my eyes to the hills from whence comes my help? My help comes from the Lord, who made heaven and earth" (Psalms 121).**

I am the ninth of thirteen children. I had eight brothers and four sisters. We had a very strong mother and father who did their best to raise us. I can't imagine how hard it must have been for my dear mother to raise so many children. I would see her on her knees at night praying for us the same way I pray for my children today.

When I was very young, I would walk long distances dreaming of what I wanted to do when I grew up. I would walk and walk until I realized that I had walked a long way from home, and then I'd get scared and turn around to go back home. One day I decided to make a clear place under a large tree in the woods behind our house, and I would go to that place and lie there and dream until I fell asleep. I would think about what I would do and places I would go when I became a woman. Later, after I was missed, one of my siblings would find me and wake me up. I was a dreamer, and to this day I still find myself dreaming.

I admired the ladies who were into jazz. I would dream that one day I would sing the same kinds of songs that my idols sang, with the sultry voices of Ms. Sarah Vaughn, Ms. Gloria Lynn, and Ms. Dakota Staten. I loved the smooth, easy style of Ms. Nancy Wilson. I couldn't get as deep as Ms. Ella Fitzgerald could, but I loved all those women and would walk and sing their songs, trying so much to imitate them. I even tried to emulate Ms. Lady Sings the Blues herself, Ms. Billie Holiday. Later I found myself falling in love with the captivating style of Ms. Nina Simon.

There was a show I would always watch called the *Ted Mack Amateur Hour*. They were looking for raw talent. I signed up and was able to get an audition. When my brother and our family friend Linwood found out what I was planning to do, they rallied around and gave me money for the bus trip. They took me to the bus stop that evening to go to Washington, DC. When I returned that night around 1:00 a.m. they were there waiting to carry me home.

I wasn't familiar with Washington, DC. I only had the address to the studio where I was to appear. I didn't have the sheet music that I needed for the piano players because I got there too late and the music stores downtown were closed. I had to stand in the middle of the floor and wing it. The man on the piano couldn't follow the song that I was singing—"Impossible" by Ms. Gloria Lynn. I didn't make it, so I came back home. All I could say was, "Well, I tried." I later learned that those ladies weren't exactly living their lives on flowerbeds of ease, either. They had big-time problems. I was so determined to go and give it a try.

I cannot explain exactly what happened to me, but I found myself getting very promiscuous after the rape. I took on many lovers to feel good. I found myself looking for something that I could not explain. I didn't really care for these guys, but I wanted to feel loved. I often tried to understand my actions and feelings. I was not sure if it was because of my father and mother's separation and my longing for him to be around. I had mixed emotions about that. My father was abusive to Mama when he drank. During the week, he was the quietest man you ever met, but come Friday through Sunday he was something else. He would get drunk and come home and take his frustrations out on our mother. I hated weekends.

When Mama finally got fed up with his abuse, she decided to make plans of her own. Her brother, Uncle Edward, gave her some land, and she hired someone to build her own little home on that land and moved us out. Now Daddy came and he lived with us, but when he started getting angry and started acting crazy, she put him out. I missed him, but I understood why she did what she did. I often thought about my father and wondered why he was so angry and abusive to my mother.

When I was very young, before I started to school, I remember living in a house on property that my father owned. One day our house burned down to the ground. To this day, my baby sister and I talk about it and still have disagreements of how it happened. Although I was very young, I remembered the entire day that it happened. My sister Ree was upstairs playing with matches and she set the house on fire.

**_"Oh Lord, hear me as I pray, pay attention to my groaning"_
(Psalm 5:1).**

I really think that my father changed when we had to live on property that belonged to Mr. Horseman, and he and my oldest brothers had to become sharecroppers. He worked in a tobacco field, and I really believe that changed him. Before then, I understood that he did his own thing. He owned his own home, earned his living doing what he wanted to do, and made a good living doing it.

I cannot remember my father being abusive to my mother until we moved. Maybe he had been that way all along, but I didn't see or hear it. Every time a fight broke out, Mama would take us with her and we would stay with our grandmother. Daddy would then come over and they would go outside and talk for hours, and Mama would take us back home. Soon she bought her own little two-room house. As time went by, she added on a few rooms, and at last we were content, or so I thought.

I don't want to make excuses for my behavior, but I was only fourteen and had that horrible experience, but it started me on a road of runaway emotions.

Now back in the day, which was around 1957, there were not many gays that I knew of. William was out and loved it, but there were so many closeted gays. There were married ones, single ones, and ones that you would never think of as being gay or thought of themselves as being gay. But if you are a man and like loving on another man, I call it gay. I had a couple of girlfriends who hated William. I couldn't figure out if they were jealous of William and my close relationship with him, or if they felt threatened by him. They would get up in his face and call him faggot and all kinds of other nasty names.

I never worried about him, because he could handle himself very well. He knew how to fight and never backed away from anyone. If someone were doing me wrong, he would challenge him or her. I never had another friend like William and I truly miss him. He passed away from AIDS.

He was a chef by trade and could cook. He moved to Baltimore and was doing very well. I left home early and lost contact with him for a time. One day he called me and told me that he had decided to move to New York City. I got worried when he told me that.

Baltimore city people were not as fast moving as New York City people, and I was afraid that they would move a little faster than William could handle. After a few years of living in New York, William came home a sick man. I don't have to tell you how hurt I was. His family took him to the Washington Hospital Center. My son Floyd and I went to visit him, and he had no idea that we were even there. He was so sick that I hardly recognized him. Shortly after, he passed away.

"Oh Lord, why do you stand so far away? Why do you hide when I need you the most?" (Psalm 10:1).

Back in those days, drugs were not something we knew about. As a matter of fact, I didn't know anything about drugs until the early sixties. William and I loved to dance, and we would drink a beer or two, but our thing was to go out and dance, dance, dance.

I joined a band when I was in high school called The Hounds. We played at high school dances and later at a few clubs. I enjoyed singing with the band and did so until I had my third child. Speedy's Wednesday night maninose night give-away began something entirely new in my life and changed it forever. "I should have danced all night!" I was trying to get away from a relationship that I should not have been in in the first place.

The man was married. I knew it but I really didn't care because I felt that I was getting as much out of it as he was, and when I got tired, I would just leave him alone. That was the norm for me: love 'em and leave 'em. Of course, he was not ready to let me go since I was such an easy mark that he could fully take advantage of, and I gave in to him willingly. But now I was getting tired of him and I no longer wanted to have casual sex with him anymore. During one of those maninose Wednesday nights, I met someone else by the name of Buddy. He was sitting in his car, and as I walked out of the bar, he called me over and started talking to me. He told me to get in and I did. He went in to get a soda and the married man saw me sitting in the car. He came over and asked me why I was in the car, and I said, "That is none of your business."

He started to reach into the car but backed off when he saw Buddy return. That was the end of that relationship and the beginning of a new one.

"Oh Lord, I have come to you for protection, don't let me be put to shame" (Psalm 31:1).

By this time I was sixteen years old, and I was madly in love. Buddy was a smooth talker, a very charismatic guy. He was down to earth, and I found it very easy to talk to him. During our conversation, I learned that he was seven years older than me. While everyone was jamming and eating in the bar, we sat in the car and talked for about two hours. He asked if he could take me home and I said yes. Well, taking me home led to driving into a wooded area and making wild, crazy love. After that was over, he took me home. Mama was up as usual but said nothing when I came in. But I later got up to use the outside toilet and found her on her knees praying.

I couldn't get enough of Buddy. I didn't want anyone else, but I soon found out that he was not exactly thinking that way. He had a main girlfriend but saw me every chance he got. To his credit, he never lied to me about her. He talked about her and told me that they had been in a relationship for a long time, although he cheated on her.

Buddy had three sons, two by the same lady and one by the one he was presently involved with. I met all three of his sons at a later time. I instantly fell in love with them because they all reminded me of their daddy, all in different ways. Neither Buddy nor I used any type of protection.

One morning Mama asked me to go to work in her place because she wasn't feeling well, so I agreed. Mama did domestic work and her employer had had a party the night before. There were a lot of dishes in the sink. I ran some water and put my hands in the warm, sudsy water and the next thing I remembered, the man was picking me up from the floor. I had fainted. That was the end of my working day. He brought me home and that evening Mama took me to the doctor. The doctor took one look at me and said, "She's pregnant." I felt like fainting again. My mother did not say a word. We left and came home.

"God is our refuge and strength, a very present help in time of trouble" (Psalm 46:1).

Those next nine months were hell. Buddy didn't want to hear that I was pregnant, and he kept his distance. His whole attitude changed. He wouldn't even talk to me about my pregnancy. He didn't want anything to do with my baby or me. As a matter of fact, word was that if I tried taking him to court, he would get some of his buddies to go to court and say that they had been intimate with me.

My son was born on November 17, 1959. I named him Floyd. He was so handsome and looked just like Buddy's other sons. They would not let me out of the hospital until I went to court and signed papers stating the name of the father. I did that and came home with my son.

One evening my mother saw Buddy at the store and she approached him. She asked him about child support. He swore to my mother that he was not the father, and she went off on him. She told him that she knew that it was his baby and he'd better be man enough to take care of it. Of course, that never happened—he never so much as brought Floyd a can of milk.

One day while I was feeding Floyd, my mother came in and said, "Mary, you know what you have to do. You got to go to work."

Back in those days, you couldn't have a baby and go back to school, so I dropped out. I felt very sad because I liked school and really missed going, and I missed some of the friends I made while going to school. I knew what I had to do when Floyd was born because I knew for sure that his father wasn't going to do anything to support him. I heard from some people that there were jobs for domestic workers in Connecticut. I talked with my mother and asked her if I could go away to work, and then send her money to support my son and help her out. She agreed, and the following month I was on my way to Connecticut.

At the age of seventeen, I found myself with a new baby and leaving home to work in another state. After a couple of days staying with some friends, I went to meet with a family that was looking for someone to take care of their child during the day. I got the job taking care of a little boy who was mentally challenged, and I fell in love with him. He had an older sister and a younger brother.

"Have mercy upon me, O God, according to thy lovingkindness: according unto the multitude of thy tender mercies blot out my transgressions" (Psalm 51:1).

I was now living with the Norris family. They lived in Greenwich, Connecticut, in a gated community. Mr. Norris worked for a TV station as an advertisement writer and Mrs. Norris was a housewife. All the domestic workers had Thursdays off, and we all would meet in Stamford, Connecticut. This is where the sisters and brothers hung out. I knew most of the folks who worked and met there, as they were all from my hometown, Calvert County, Maryland. We would eat breakfast then all go our separate ways.

I bought things for my baby, got my hair fixed, shopped a little for myself, and got a money order to send to Mama. We would later meet and decide what we were going to do later that evening. Some of us would get together and go to New York, and some would stay in Stamford and party at the clubs there.

I met this fellow by the name of Sonny Mayes. Sonny was a fine, very good-looking man. He was soft spoken, with a thick mustache, light brown in complexion, and he dressed very well. We became close. Sonny treated me with respect. He knew I was young and just coming from the country, so he taught me things, like how to take care of my body and keep my body smelling good. He had all kinds of good-smelling things. The only problem was that Sonny was a drug addict. He would take me to his apartment and I would sit on the couch and watch him beat his bongo and nod. After about an hour or so, he would walk me to the train station and see that I got on the train back to Greenwich. He didn't try to take me to bed for a long time, and when we did, he was very gentle.

Several times he and I would be walking to his place, and I would notice this policeman standing at an intersection of Pacific Street in Stamford. Later I saw that he would follow us, and sometimes he would follow us all the way home to Sonny's place.

I later found out that he and Sonny knew each other, and the officer would sometimes come by the apartment and visit for a while, then leave. This happened a few times. I never thought much of it. I just assumed they understood each other. I am sure he knew Sonny was an addict.

I made friends easily with all the folks that I met. One night I rode to New York City with some guys. There were about six of us. I noticed that all of them, except for the driver, were anxious and talked fast. When we got to New York, I was told to wait at this place for them and they would be right back. I noticed that I was standing in front of a photo shop. I went in and had some pictures taken so I could send them home to my family. I never was afraid waiting for the guys to return. After about thirty minutes, they returned and we went back to Connecticut. The guys were all laughing and happy. It never occurred to me that I was in any danger, as I had met the driver through my friend Ann. She liked him and introduced me to him. The next day I told Ann what happened and she went off on me.

"Girl, what were you thinking going to New York with a bunch of dope addicts? Don't you know they went to New York to buy drugs and get high? If the police had stopped him, guess who would have ended up with all the drugs on them? You!"

(Angel watching over me!)

Well, that was the last time I made that trip, but I had some nice pictures taken and sent them home.

After I realized that Sonny was more interested in drugs than me, we went our separate ways. I would see him on the corner sometimes nodding. I felt so sorry for him because he was so good looking to have lived that way. I never knew what happened to him. Ann was in love with another fine-looking man, who I found out later was also a heroin addict. He knew Sonny and would tell me how he was doing for a time, but then he also disappeared out of Ann's life.

During the week and on weekends, I would take care of the Norris children. Sometimes I would cook and put clothes in the washer, but most of the time I spent taking care of the little boy. Although I would show love to the children, when I went to my room at night, I would cry myself to sleep. My body would ache for my baby. I had never in my life felt that kind of pain, a pain that I wouldn't wish on my worst enemy. I missed Floyd so much.

I would get the chance to go home for a while and spend time with him, and then return to Connecticut. I could not get the look of my baby's eyes out of my mind when I was about to leave him. I cried so much at night just to hold him in my arms and kiss his little handsome face. My dear mother never complained. She also loved him very much. I can now imagine how she felt when I think of how much I love my grandchildren.

When I returned to Connecticut, I would go through the motions of spending my days off in Stamford, getting my hair done, taking photos, and spending time with Ann, Delores, Robert Bell and his wife Rose, George Gantt, Winfield King, and my cousin Gertrude Bowen. We all were from Calvert County. This was 1960 when Smokey Robinson and the Miracles were singing, "Shop Around." I loved that song.

One day I went into a little sandwich shop to get something to eat and met this guy standing in there. He was very dark complexed, with his hair fried, dyed, and laid to the side. He spoke to me and we began to talk. He said his name was Peter Saunders. He had a smile that would melt your heart. I should have turned and walked away, but I didn't. It wasn't long before we were dating. In the beginning, Pete, as everyone called him, was very nice, but later I noticed that he was becoming controlling. He really didn't want me to be with anyone else but him. He wasn't impressed when I spoke of my son. I showed him a picture of Floyd and he called him peasy head. That didn't go over too well with me, but I just dismissed it.

There was a club called Bobby Oasis Bar & Grill that was located on Pacific Street in Stamford where we all ate breakfast in the morning and partied at night. One night, Pete and I were standing at the bar and this guy that I would see periodically came up and said, "Hey, black Pete." He then put his arm around my shoulder and said, "Hi, baby." Before the word *baby* barely got out of his mouth, Pete hit him so hard I felt the wind from his fist when it came past my head. As a matter of fact, it touched the side of my face. They fought into the street. I am not sure who won the fight, but I remembered it was terrible.

During those days, I was young, I was stacked, and I had big legs and nice hips—the kind that men admired. I don't know if that made Pete angry or just plain jealous. He became very abusive toward me after that.

"Though a host should encamp against me, my heart shall not fear: though war should rise against me, in this will I be confident" (Psalm 27:3).

One night Pete came to pick me up and he met Mrs. Norris. He was so polite I hardly recognized him. Of course Mrs. Norris thought he was nice, but I knew better by then. He had on this long, black leather coat and his hair was neatly done. Back in those days some men would get their hair straightened and waved, called "conk."

One night he took me to Harlem in New York to see Jackie Wilson perform. We went to the Apollo Theater. That was the first time I had ever been to a show and I enjoyed it. Pete became very annoyed because I was clapping and really enjoying the show. Jackie Wilson, singing and dancing, was so smooth. Pete leaned over to me and said, "I guess if he wanted to take you to bed, you would let him." I felt so bad and thought, *If he is so jealous, why would he even bring me here?*

Pete became more possessive as time went by. He wanted me to go everywhere with him instead of being with my friends on my days off. He played amateur football, and I had to go to the stadium to watch him play even though it was cold. I had to go to the salon and wait while he got his hair done. I couldn't hang with my friends on my nights off. I had to be with him. After a while that got very old and I started to lose my feelings for him.

One morning I decided I was going to eat with my friends. On that Thursday morning, Ann, Delores, Rose, and I were eating breakfast in a club called Oasis when Pete came to the door and beckoned me to come out. He said, "I thought I told you not to go in there."

I said, "Peter, we are eating breakfast. What's wrong with that?"

He said, "Come on, I'll show you what's wrong with it." He threw me in the car, took me around the block, got out of his car, went into the trunk and got a brush that you wash your car tires with, and beat me with it.

After he finished beating my body and face, he went across the street to the drugstore and bought alcohol and bandages. He took me to his brother's house to patch me up. I wish that I could say this was the last time he beat me, but it wasn't. He beat me another night because a car full of guys drove by when Pete and I had just left a restaurant. One of the guys made a howling sound, and Pete smiled at him in a way of saying, "Yes, she is all mine." He said, "Yes, that's how all those niggers feel, but you belong to me." When I didn't respond, he reached around and slapped me in the face.

When we got home, he wanted to take me to bed. That was his way of explaining how much he loved me and why he did what he did. He would always say, "You know, when a man loves a woman, he just can't help but be jealous." I hated him, but I was afraid to leave him for fear of what he would do to me. So I decided to stop going into town on my days off for a while. He came to the house and promised me that he would never hit me again, and I believed him.

I will never forget one night when Peter and I went to this club. The music was good and I was in a good mood. I turned around and there was Sonny Mayes standing there looking good. He spotted me and came over to say hello. He asked me how I was doing. Before I could reply, Peter came up and put his arms around me and said, "She's doing fine!"

Sonny smiled and said, "It's nice to see you, Mary."

I said, "Thanks, Sonny, it's good to see you too."

Of course I had to hear Peter putting him down the rest of the evening. He called Sonny all kinds of things—junkie, dope user, and every negative name he could think of. But there is one thing I knew, and still know until this day. Sonny treated me with great respect. He always treated me like a lady. He taught me how to respect my body and keep it clean. He knew I was young when he met me, and there were things I didn't know.

Sonny taught me so much as a young girl that I will never forget him no matter what others thought of him. He was a good man who had a drug addiction. I don't know what happened to Sonny because I never saw him again. I didn't go into town for a while. I needed to get away from Peter.

He came over one day and I saw his car pull up outside. I was home alone. He rang the doorbell and then knocked for a while when I didn't answer. I watched as he sat in his car, and then he left because he probably thought I was out with the Norris family.

The house that I lived in was very large. I lived in part of the house that had a long hallway that I had to walk to get to the main part of the house. It was like my separate apartment. One night, about a week later, I was getting ready to go to bed when I heard a knock at my door. I figured it was Mrs. Norris so I opened the door and found Pete standing there. He came in and said, "What's going on? You trying to get away from me?" I started to say no when I heard this click. I looked and saw this long switchblade knife he had opened. He put the knife to my neck.

I started to cry and begged him not to hurt me. I said, "Please, Peter, don't hurt me. I have a child at home. Please don't hurt me!"

After he watched me cry for a minute, he put the knife away and said, "I wasn't going to hurt you. I just want to know if you are trying to leave me." Then he put me on the bed and had sex with me. That was his routine. I was too scared not to comply, but I felt nothing but hate for him.

The next morning, I told Mrs. Norris about it and asked her to never let him in the house again. After that night, I was really scared of Peter because I knew that he was capable of really doing me great harm. I stayed away from Stamford for a while and stayed close to the house.

(Angel watching over me!)

"I will praise you, Lord, for you have rescued me. You refused to let my enemies triumph over me" (Psalm 30:1).

One evening I decided to go into town to see if I would see any of my friends, but no one was around. I ate dinner, and when I came out, I found that I had missed my train. There would not be another going my way for a few hours. I was really disturbed because I knew no one and felt very alone. The policeman who had followed Sonny and me around was standing on the corner. He saw me and asked if anything was wrong.

I was almost in tears and told him that I had missed my train and had to wait around for another one. He told me that he would be getting off in about a half hour and would take me home. He told me to sit in the restaurant and wait for him. Shortly, he came by and got me. He drove me back to Greenwich, Connecticut. On the way, he told me that he wanted so much to meet me and talk with me, but he had seen me with Sonny and later with Peter. He said he wanted to tell me to get away from Peter because he was bad news. But he did not want to get in my business. He was very kind and very handsome. I noticed that he had a nice smile and beautiful teeth.

It was December and the snow was deep. I had never experienced snow that deep, although I came from the country. I was told that snowdrifts were maddening in New York and Connecticut, and I found that out.

When we got to the house, we sat in the car for hours and talked. I loved being with him and really didn't want to leave. He asked me if he could kiss me. We kissed and kissed. He told me that he had wanted to do that for a long time. We made love that night in his car. I never felt like that before. He was gentle and kind with me, and the loving was so good. We went to sleep in each other's arms. He would start the car and let it get warm, and then turn it off again. He did that for hours. Finally, we said good-bye and I never saw him again.

A few weeks later, I got together with some of my friends and we decided to go shopping. We went into a store and I wanted to buy some cologne. At that time, My Sin perfume was popular. I picked up a bottle, sprayed some, and got violently sick. I threw up everywhere. That was the day I realized I was indeed pregnant.

Oh, my Lord, what in the world was I going to do? I left home to make life better for my son, and now I find myself pregnant again. *What am I going to do?* Being pregnant was not as frightening as thinking, *Who is the father? I had sex with Peter and I also had sex with the policeman. Who is the father of this baby?* I went into town and met with Peter.

He was surprisingly nice and took me out to dinner. On my way back home, I told him that I was pregnant. Naturally, he thought the baby was his. I told him that I was going to go home for a while and tell my mother. I told Mrs. Norris that I was pregnant and I wanted to go home. She understood, told me that it was okay, and wished me luck with my pregnancy. I went home to be with my son.

"In thee, O Lord, do I put my trust; let me never be ashamed: deliver me in thy righteousness" (Psalm 31:1).

When I told my mother she never scolded me or said anything negative. She was supportive and took care of me. I got a job at the maninose house and went to work every day, until the morning I woke and started to get ready for work and a pain hit me in the back. Later that day, Juan, my second son, was born.

During my pregnancy, my sister Susie was also pregnant with her daughter. I will never forget it. One night I caught a ride with her then boyfriend, Conroy. Later she married him. I was at this bar called Spinning Wheel. My brother David and a friend of ours named Linwood worked there. It was the spot that everyone went to. I loved going there to dance, see people, and listen to music. At that time, it was the only place to go other than Speedy's. This bar/club was black-owned by two men from Virginia. They brought excitement to the place. I sang there one night with the band that I started with in high school. There was entertainment brought from Washington, DC.

Billy Stewart was one of the main attractions to entertain there. This particular night was slow and no one was there except David and Linwood, who often spent the night there. It was getting late and I wondered if anyone would show up that I could get a ride with. Just before the place closed, Conroy stopped in and I caught a ride home with him. I had no idea that he was as drunk as he was until we got to the corner store, just below where I lived. He stopped the car at the corner, dropped his head, and went to sleep. I got out of the car to walk up the road to my house when a couple of Susie's children came up to the car and found him asleep. I told them that he gave me a ride. I left them there with him and walked up the road to home.

They went home and got my sister Susie and told her that I was riding with him, and then I went home. Later that night, I was in bed almost asleep when Susie came storming in telling Mama that she wanted to talk to me. She came in the room and asked me if I with Conroy. I told her that I caught a ride with him from Spinning Wheel. I told her that I didn't know he was as drunk as he was. I said, "As soon as he stopped at the corner store, he went to sleep." I was amused and laughed, but she wasn't laughing. She went on and on about being in the car with him. When I realized that she was accusing me of being with him, I told her that I would never do anything like that to her, but she did not believe me.

We went most of that summer riding in the same car to work without her saying a word to me. I was so hurt because Susie and I were always very close. I loved her so much, and I missed our relationship. She was convinced that I was messing around with her man. Susie gave birth to her daughter, Nan, and later that summer I gave birth to Juan. When I brought my son home from the hospital, Susie came to the house to see him. She took one look at him and said, "Oh, Mary, he is so pretty." She had a relieved look on her face. That is when I realized that she thought my baby belonged to her man.

From that day on, she and I were friends again. We talked, and I told her that I would never have done that to her, and especially with him. I was so angry with him because I felt that he wanted her to think that there was something going on with us. I didn't have any respect for him because he did not treat my sister right, and I felt that he never really did love her the way she loved him. To this day, I feel that he was responsible for my sister's death. One day her blood pressure went up so high that the doctor could not get it down and she passed away.

As far back as I could remember, although Susie was much older than I was, we were very close. I was the ninth and Susie was the second of thirteen siblings. When I would visit her, she would be so happy to see me and we always had nice visits. We were best friends, and I miss my older sister very much. When I think about it, I regret how much time was lost during that entire summer of not speaking to each other. She used to talk to me about everything, and I knew she was unhappy. She and I always enjoyed each other's company. When we were estranged that whole summer, it really broke my heart. When she saw that Juan looked nothing like she thought he would look, she knew that it was not possible for him to belong to her man. However, I also had a realization. I also knew that he was in no way the son of Peter Saunders and I was thrilled about that. I knew that the policeman was his father.

The thing that hurts me to the core of my being, and still to this day makes me cry sometimes at night, is knowing that my son was cheated of his father.

Seeing him go through some of the things that he went through, and probably is still experiencing to this day, really breaks my heart, because I feel that it is my fault and there is nothing that I can do or could have done about it.

I pray often to God for forgiveness. One night as I was crying and praying and asking God to forgive me, I heard the Holy Spirit reply, "I have already forgiven you; you need to forgive yourself." I felt that presence, and I felt a sense of relief immediately. To this day, I can still feel the hurt and pain that I have caused, especially when I see my son. He has never said one word to me about his father. I believe that he may not have wanted to offend me, so he never questioned me about him.

He now has three sons of his own, and I see that he really doesn't know how to deal with them on a certain level as a father because he never had one of his own. He told my daughter that he really doesn't know how to be a father. When his sons were growing up, he spent most of the time in jail because of selling drugs and later using them. Most of his young adult life, while his children were growing up, he was not around to raise them or get to know them.

I can't tell you how much I have beaten myself up and cried at night because I feel that I have cheated my son Juan out of having, or even knowing, his father. I feel because of that, he was confused and really didn't know how to handle the whole situation, but he didn't want to blame me. He loves me so much that he is determined to spare my feelings. His father never knew that I was pregnant by him, either, because I left Connecticut and never spoke to him again.

Now that Juan's boys are grown and have children of their own, I can see his sons following the same pattern as their father. They are going back and forth to jail for bad decisions they are making in their lives. There are times that I think of trying to locate Juan's father by hiring someone who will find him. I hesitate in doing that because I am not sure if he is still living, if he has a family, or if he would even acknowledge the fact that he remembered me.

I wrote a letter to my cousin who was still living in Stamford, Connecticut, at the time and told her about my son and the policeman. She wrote back and told me that she knew whom I was talking about because she dated him for a time. She said his name was Albert Morris. When we talked the night we were together, he told me his name was Albert, but folks called him Duke. My cousin told me that he left the Stamford Connecticut Police Department because he was accused of selling drugs to folks, then arresting them. She said that he went to live in New York and got on the police force there, but had gotten in some more trouble. She told me that his picture was all over the newspapers for wrongdoing. She stated that the last she heard of Albert, he had gotten married and had moved to Macon, Georgia. After I received that letter, I wasn't sure if I even wanted my son to know his father, or if I even wanted to find him.

"I will bless the Lord at all times: his praise shall continually be in my mouth. My soul shall make her boast in the Lord: the humble shall hear thereof, and be glad" (Psalm 34:1–2).

When Juan got locked up, I sent him the letter that I received from my cousin. I wanted him to read it and waited for his reply, but he never replied. He brought the letter back when he was released from jail. I have it in my personal box and maybe one day we will talk about it.

When I left Connecticut, I never returned. I spoke with Peter on the phone a few times and he sent clothes for the baby, but I never saw him again. And unfortunately, I never saw the policeman, either. Now at the age of eighteen and a half, I was the mother of two. I wanted to display the letter that my cousin wrote to me dated May 1, 1984.

> *Mary,*
>
> *I received your letter on Saturday and was glad to hear from you, was also glad to see you Easter Sunday, since it has been years since I've seen you.*
>
> *I am sorry that you have had to carry this burden around with you all these years. I can imagine what it has done to you and how you must feel that you could not tell your son what he really wanted to know.*
>
> *Duke, Albert Morris, got in trouble in drugs. Would sell the stuff, then he would have the guys busted. The police department knew all of this but never did anything for a long time. Finally, they made him take a medical leave of absence. He spent time in the psychiatric ward. There was nothing mentally wrong with him in that respect, but they had to make it look good! Next thing I know there is this big write-up in New York and Connecticut papers with his picture halfway across the page where he had been arrested for dealing in drugs in New York and Connecticut.*
>
> *He was cleared of that. Then his picture appeared in the papers again, where he had been connected in the killing of a Norwalk detective who was also known as a drug dealer. He went to court, was held, but I never heard anything else until we went to Macon, Georgia and Martin, he's my husband, went to visit one of his uncles and came back to*

the house and surprised me with the news of seeing Duke, and that he had asked for me.

Martin told him that he thought that he was still in New York. He told Martin that they couldn't prove that he had killed that detective. But you know he killed a guy in front of Bobby Oasis, shot him in the back, and so I don't put anything past him. We dated about 8 months, but he was very attentive to me. He married a young girl named Cheryl.

The last I heard, they were still in Macon, Georgia. The life he has led has been one of drugs and murder from what I have read in the papers. This is about six years ago. Hope I have given you some insight on Albert Morris, the cop, killer, and drug dealer. Write me soon.

Love,

Gertrude

"Oh Lord, rebuke me not in thy wrath: neither chasten me in thy hot displeasure" (Psalm 38:1).

Wow! After I received that letter, I didn't know what to do. I felt with a history like that, it would probably be better not to find Juan's father, so I didn't try.

The following summer I received a letter from my friend Ann, whom I spent a lot of time with while in Connecticut. Ann told me that Peter was dead. She ask if I wanted to come back for his funeral. I told her no and asked her what had happened to him. Ann said that Peter was what you called a number backer. He took money from folks who placed bets on numbers. A person who placed a bet with him had won a lot of money, but Peter did not pay him. He avoided this person for a time. However, one day the man found him talking with someone in a telephone booth and left him there with a knife in his heart.

My feelings at the time were "you reap what you sow, you get what you deserve." Peter was a very abusive man and treated others poorly. Sometimes I felt that he didn't like women very much, and really didn't like people, period. I don't know, and will never know, how many women he abused, but I am willing to bet that I wasn't the only one he beat on. In a way I felt relieved when I heard that he was no longer walking among us.

After having my second son, Juan, on July 22, 1961, I was feeling and looking good. My body was in good shape, and my clothes were once again looking good on me. I went out with some friends one day and stopped at this bar. Buddy pulled up. He came over and spoke to me. By this time, I was very much over him and he knew it. With the terrible way he treated me, I was not interested in him in any way. He didn't attract me at all. I walked away from him and ignored him the entire time. We all stood out in the yard and had fun. Being the playboy that he was didn't stop him from trying to sweet talk me whenever he saw me. I was looking good and I knew it.

Buddy did all he could to spark my interest in him, but nothing would change my mind about him. He never mentioned his son Floyd. It was as though he didn't exist.

One day I was out with William, as he would pick me up sometimes just to get me out of the house. My sister loved to babysit for me so I went out that day. William and I stopped at this club called Duke's. It was around two o'clock in the afternoon and there were a few people in the club. Buddy came in and stood at the bar for a while. Later, he came over to the table where William and I sat and asked me to come outside. He wanted to talk with me, but I refused. He told me that he wasn't going to ask me again, so he said, "Get up and come outside." I again refused. He grabbed me by the arm and pulled me outside, and then threw me in the car. By the time William came over to the car to open the door, Buddy had pulled off. He carried me down the road and pulled into a long dirt road and a vacant area. He pushed me down, pulled my underclothes off, and raped me. I cried and ask him to stop, but he said, "You trying to be cute with me? I'll show you." When he finished, he pulled his zipper up on his pants, drove me back to the bar, and told me to get out.

William was standing outside when we got back. Buddy got out of the car and William jumped into his face to fight, but Buddy told him if he tried to hit him, he would kill him. I told William that we should get away from there. I told him what happened and William asked me if I was going to tell anyone. I told him no. Everyone knew how crazy I once was about him and no one would believe me anyway.

"Fret not thyself because of evildoers, neither be thou envious against the workers of iniquity. For they shall soon be cut down like the grass and wither as the green herb" (Psalm 37:1–2).

A month or so later, I was eating a peach and got violently ill. Well, I discovered later that I was once again pregnant. I could not believe it, and what really made me ill was, not only was I pregnant again, but I was pregnant by Buddy again. I was so depressed I didn't know what to do. There was one thing I knew I had to do, and that was to tell Mama. Mama did not complain, argue, or make me feel bad. She stood by me as always.

I also told William. He asked me what was I going to do, and I said, "I don't know." He asked if I was going to tell Buddy, and I said, "No, he wouldn't care or own it anyway." I wanted to commit suicide a number of times, I felt so bad, but I had two other sons I had to think about.

Later when William saw Buddy, he jumped all up in his face and cursed him out. He called Buddy all kinds of no good so-and-sos and was ready to fight. Buddy told him to get out of his face, and he told him what he was going to do to him. William was not scared.

A lot of folks really underestimate gay guys. They think that because they are gay, they can't fight or take care of themselves. They forget that they are still men. William was one that neither men nor women wanted to challenge when it came to fighting, William could take care of himself. I loved him and I miss him terribly.

I would think that when women get pregnant, it is supposed to be one of the best feelings they could have, yet I was depressed every time I got pregnant. Buddy would see me and act as though he didn't see me. I never said anything to him and he said nothing to me. Around the time I was to deliver my baby, in the month of October, Buddy was planning his wedding.

I went to the store and bought a set of beautiful glasses and sent them to his bride. Speaking of his bride, we knew each other, and she knew her soon-to-be husband was a womanizer, but she loved him, and for some reason she also liked me too. She would always compliment me and say, "Girl, I wish I had those big legs you have."

She understood that I was young and vulnerable, and she also knew that Buddy was after me and it was just one sided. So she and I never had bad feelings toward each other. I delivered my third son, Gregg, on October 21, 1963. During my pregnancy with Gregg, I continued to sing with the band that I had started with called The Hounds. There wasn't a lot of work to be had in Calvert County, so I had to work when and where I could. During the weekends, I made a little money, enough to feed my children and buy whatever they needed.

Of course I had the help of my mother and other members of my family. There were times my sister would babysit for me to give me a break. One night I was at Spinning Wheel and met a guy who was visiting from Washington, DC. His name was Leroy. We were attracted to one another and began to see each other on a regular basis when he would come down on weekends.

Leroy was fun to be with. He laughed a lot and made me laugh. I liked him a lot. After about three months of coming down, he decided to tell me that he was married. My heart was broken because I could not believe that he could get away as often as he did to see me and be married. I stopped seeing Leroy for a time when he would come down. I would pretend that I was not home and would not go out on the weekends for a while, although I missed seeing him.

One of the men that he would travel with came down on a Saturday night and told me that Leroy had gotten arrested and was in the DC jail. I wrote him and told him that I was sorry that he was locked up, and that I wanted to see him and talk with him upon his release. That was a relationship that I knew was wrong, but I continued it anyway.

I tried to find work, but there were no jobs in Calvert County. I spoke with our pastor's wife. They lived in Washington, DC. She told me that I could get a job with the government, but I had to come there and put in an application. I spoke to Mama about it. She said if I could find a job in DC, she would take care of the boys.

There was a family that came down on weekends to party at Spinning Wheel. I got to know them well. They were Linny, Elijah, and Viola Mackall. I spoke to Linny and expressed that I would like to come to DC and find a job. She told me that I could stay with them and she would help me find one. The next weekend, I packed up some clothes and went back to DC with the Mackalls. Viola was Elijah's daughter—Linny's step-daughter. She was cool to live with. I tried to find work any place that I could, because I did not want to live there for free. I started to work at a laundry pulling sheets. After one week, I had to give that up because the work was too hard, and

I would be so tired when I got off. I just wanted to sleep, sometimes without eating dinner.

My second job was working at a drugstore that was located on the 1900 block of Pennsylvania Avenue at the lunch counter. It was located directly across from George Washington University and was busy all the time. A lot of the students from the college would come and sit at the lunch counter. I noticed this young white boy each time he came in. He would sit at the counter where I was working and smile at me all the time. Sometimes he would stand around until a seat became available just to sit where I was. He came in every day. One day after I took his order, I talked with him.

He told me that he was from Boston, Massachusetts, and a freshman at the university. He told me that he had a crush on me. I smiled, but I really didn't take him seriously. One day he came in with a dozen roses for me and a card that said, "Happy Valentine to the one that I adore!" Naturally, the girls behind the counter started to tease me. He came in one evening when I was getting off from work and asked if he could walked me to the bus stop.

I thanked him for the card and roses and told him that I really appreciated all that he had done, but I couldn't have any kind of a relationship with him. I told him how old I was and that I was the mother of three children. He looked hurt. I gave him a big hug and got on the bus. I didn't see him for a while. Then one day when I came to work, there was a card that he had left for me. Inside was a certificate for two hundred dollars to one of the department stores downtown. His note said that he was sorry that we couldn't have a relationship and he was returning home. I never saw him again. I went to Garfunkel's and bought a pink skirt and a sweater to match.

I continued to see Leroy, although I was getting tired of the relationship. Leroy loved to drink. I once thought it was fun, but now it wasn't as amusing, and I was not feeling good about dealing with him. After all, he was a married man.

Lenny and Elijah lived on 3rd and New York Avenue, right on the bus route. Across the street from where we lived was a gas station. Black folks ran this station. I would sit on the steps and watch the cars come and go. Sometimes I would walk across the street to the station and buy a soda or a bag of chips. There was a guy working as a mechanic named Curtis. Curtis talked a lot and was old school. He called women bitches. He would talk about women, and laugh and smile while calling them bitches. He seemed very comfortable calling women bitches. I later realized that it was a term of endearment, and the women he called bitches answered and enjoyed him calling them that. But the one thing I noticed about Curtis was that he always treated me with respect, and I never heard him refer to me as a bitch.

In order for me to get home from work after I got off the bus, I had to walk across the gas station's yard, and Curtis would always be standing around with a cloth in his hands. He worked on cars and was always greasy and dirty. When he was finished working for the day, he would go into the bathroom and clean up. He would come out clean with his slacks and hat matching. He cleaned up well. Getting to know Curtis was hilarious, and it was the first time I was introduced to marijuana.

One evening, Curtis picked up his girlfriend Toni and they came by and took me for a ride with them. I was sitting in the back seat when he passed me this thing that looked like a cigarette. At first I told him that I didn't smoke cigarettes. Toni told me that it was a little different from a cigarette and would make me feel good and mellow. I took it and started to smoke it. Curtis and Toni later laughed at me all evening because I was talking and singing, the music on the radio sounded so good. Everything looked and felt different. I loved that feeling. I made it my business to find it every chance I got.

"Have mercy upon me, O God, according to thy loving-kindness: according unto the multitude of thy tender mercies blot out my transgressions. Wash me thoroughly from mine iniquity, and cleanse me from my sin" (Psalm 51:1–2).

One evening as I was walking across the station's yard, this tall, good-looking, pretty-eyed guy walked up to me and introduced himself. His name was Herbert. Herbert was smooth and slick and easy to look at. He had a way about him when he talked. He had this smile on his face and his head would tilt to one side. I liked him from the beginning. I would notice the expressions on Curtis's face when he saw Herbert talking to me. At the time, I didn't understand why, but I later understood. Curtis knew him well, but I didn't. Herbert would come across the street when he saw me sitting on the steps. This became a regular thing and I looked forward to seeing him.

I was still seeing Leroy now and then. We would go out to eat, or to a movie or a show. Leroy was a lot of fun and he made me laugh a lot. I really enjoyed being with him, although I also looked forward to seeing Herbert, and I found myself seeing both of them. Sometimes, Herbert would get his father's car and pick me up at my job. We would ride around sometimes, and at other times we would go to a motel and make love.

One evening, Herbert picked me up and took me to a house where there were folks gambling. I remembered sitting in the living room while the men were in another room shooting craps. This went on most of the night. He would periodically check on me to see if I wanted or needed anything. I fell asleep and woke up to rumbling sounds coming from where they were. A fight had broken out, and it was Herbert and another man who had claimed Herbert was cheating with bad dice. Someone broke up the fight and Herbert and his friend came out and told me to come on, they were leaving. By that time, it was morning. We left and went to get something to eat.

Herbert was talking to his friend. I was in the back seat. He was talking about going home to get some money and he slipped and said, "I know when I ask Brenda for some money, she is going to raise hell as usual." All of a sudden, they both looked back at me and saw a look on my face that revealed I was surprised to hear that he was married. Herbert reached back to take my hand, but I snatched it back and told him that I wanted to go home. After he found that I didn't want to talk, they drove me home. I was so hurt. There I go again, falling for another married man. I could not believe he was married because we had spent so much time together. We were seeing each other almost every day.

I hadn't seen him for about a week when he came across the street one evening when he saw me sitting on the steps. He wanted to take me for a ride in his father's car, but I refused, so we sat on the steps and talked for a long time. He told me how sorry he was and thought that I knew he was married because he figured that Curtis had told me as he had threatened to do. He ran this long story down to me—how unhappy he and his wife were, and that he was in the process of moving out, and on and on. Old gullible me fell hook, line, and sinker and forgave him, and we went to a motel and made passionate love that evening. Meanwhile, I was still seeing Leroy now and then.

Later one Friday evening after work, some of the girls and I decided that we wanted to get a fish dinner. We went over to this carry-out restaurant located on Benning Road. When I walked in to the carry-out, I smelled the fish cooking and got violently sick. I had to run outside and throw up. That's how I found out that I was pregnant. Nine months later, on April 4, 1965, I delivered my daughter Lori. She was born in DC General Hospital.

The night before Lori was born, Leroy and I had made love. After he left, I drank a bottle of wine all by myself. Around two or three o'clock in the morning, I decided to get into the bathtub and take a long bubble bath. As soon as I got out, I felt this sharp pain in my back and I knew that she was coming. A friend of mine by the name of Bessie had a feeling that I was ready to go, so earlier that evening she told me to call her at any hour and she would get a cab to take me to the hospital.

I called Bessie and told her that I was ready. About fifteen minutes later a cab was honking for me and Bessie was in it. I wasn't at the hospital long before I delivered. As a matter of fact, they told me to take a shower. I tried to tell them that I had just gotten out of the bathtub, but they insisted that I take a shower. I was hurting so bad that I had to hold my stomach to keep from having the baby in the shower. As soon as they came to put me on the table to roll me into the delivery room, I spread my legs wide open and pushed. They tried to keep me from doing that, but I told them that my baby was ready to come out and she did. By the time they got me in the delivery room, Lori was lying on my stomach. She was a frisky little thing, just as pretty as she could be and already with a mind of her own. When I brought her home, she had one hand on her cheek with her legs crossed.

I was both happy and confused. I really believed that I knew when I had gotten pregnant with Lori, and I knew that Herbert was her father. However, I was also having sex with Leroy and he believed that she was his. He even gave Lori her middle name. I had already told him that I wanted to name her Lori. I had seen a soap opera and a girl by the name of Lori was on it, so I said if I ever have a daughter, I would name her Lori. Leroy told me to name her Lori Burnette, so I did.

"I waited patiently for the Lord; and he inclined unto me, and heard my cry. He brought me up also out of a horrible pit, out of the miry clay, and set my feet upon a rock, and established my goings" (Psalm 40:1–2).

Before I gave birth to Lori, I didn't say too much to either men, because deep down I really didn't know who the father was. I believed in my heart of hearts that I knew when I had conceived her. I had felt it as soon as it happened. But I decided to wait until my baby was born. At first glance, I knew Herbert was her father. She had his eyes, nose, and bone structure.

After Lori was born, I went home. Again, my mother took her and loved her so much.

(Angel watching over me!)

In the beginning, I mentioned that I was a promiscuous girl. I guess by this time you would say that I am more than that! After all, I have four children by three different men. While writing this, I realized that my situation was like someone on drugs looking for that initial high, but never finding it. So I go on and on trying to feel it and find it, but never could. Something was missing in my life that I felt I couldn't replace.

A week later, Leroy came down to see Lori. His first look let him know that the baby was not his. We talked and I told him about Herbert. He couldn't get too angry. After all, he was a married man. Needless to say, our relationship was not the same, although we saw each other every now and then when he came down to my home, but it was just not the same for either of us.

Herbert now sort of kept his distance, and we never really discussed Lori, although he knew that she was his. I would walk across the gas station's yard with her in a stroller to take her to the clinic, but he never said anything. I felt that part of that was my fault for not knowing whose baby she was from the beginning, so I never said anything to him about her being his child. But when he saw her, he knew that she was his child.

Again, I took my baby home to my mother, and it was not long before I was off to Washington, DC, to find work, as there was no work to be found at home. My dear mother told me that she would take care of Lori. She made a bed out of a large box with two pillows and laid Lori in it. That was Lori's bed and she looked comfortable lying in that homemade bed.

I did not stay at Lenny's much longer. She decided that I was having too much fun with Leroy, so she decided to take the door off my bedroom. I felt that she was getting a little too personal, so I decided to find somewhere else to live. I went to work at a club located on H Street, NW, not too far from where I was staying. I worked as a waitress for a while, but then I heard that the police department was hiring crossing guards, so I applied for that job and got it.

All I had to do was come down to the street and work once in the morning when children were going to school and once in the afternoon when they got out of school. Of course that job didn't pay much, and I really didn't have much money to live on or to send home. One of the ladies I worked with, Rose, told me that she had an apartment right up the street and I could stay there for free. She stayed with her boyfriend most of the time and only stayed at the apartment sometimes on weekends.

Rose took her job seriously. She marched like she was in the army. When she blew her whistle standing in the middle of the street to stop the cars and let the children cross the street, she was serious. We often laughed and joked with Rose about her seriousness. Rose took a liking to me. She told me that she liked me because I was real. She would say, "Girl, I like you because what you see is what you get. There is nothing phony about you."

One morning I overslept and heard a knock at the door. When I opened it, this big, burly, black policeman was standing there. He told me that I was late and he had to direct traffic. I told him that I was sorry and I would get ready. I tried to close the door, but he put his foot in the door and held it opened. He came in and tried to put his arms around me. I pushed him away and threatened that I would report him, so he stopped and left. During orientation, the chief of police told us that he would protect us at any cost, and if we encountered any problems, to come to him and let him know. So that is just what I did. It wasn't long before that big guy was gone. I don't know if he was fired or just transferred, but I didn't see him again.

After I was through working for the day as a crossing guard, I would go into the club and work in the kitchen for a few hours just to make some extra money. One day as I was sitting at the bar, a man came in and ordered a soda. He started talking to me and I noticed that he was handsome and had a nice smile. We talked for a while. After that day, he showed up every day and we became very close. He started to come up to the apartment that I was staying in and spending some nights with me. I was not happy where I was staying because of the many roaches in that place, but I couldn't complain because I wasn't paying any rent. When you turned off the lights, they would come out, and then scatter when the lights came on. I wasn't used to that, as we didn't have roaches at home. My mother would never allow it. She kept her home very clean.

It wasn't long before Rose told me that she was getting married and letting the apartment go. I knew that I had to make other arrangements. I couldn't go back and stay with the Mackalls because Elijah's sister, Irene, was a bit angry with me because of a guy I met by the name of Norman. One evening we were sitting on the steps and this guy came by and stopped. He got out of the car and walked up. Irene introduced us. Although she was married, Irene hung out and did pretty much as she wanted to do. She and Norman had a previous relationship, but at that time, it was over. But Irene was the kind of girl who wanted to claim and hold on to her old lovers. Norman kept his eyes on me and I kept mine on him. He would stop by when he saw me sitting on the steps some evenings. He ask me to go out, but I told him that I wouldn't do Irene like that. He told me that he and Irene didn't have anything going; they were just friends.

So I started to go out with Norman. Irene heard about it and got angry with me. After that I knew that I had to move because I was, after all, living with her family.

So I moved out and got a room over the club where I worked part time. I dated Norman for a long time, off and on, but he was creeping around and lying about it, so I didn't want to get too involved with him. I kept him at a distance, but we dated for a while.

The beginning of my relationship with Marshall Brown happened one day while I was sitting at the bar. He came in, spoke to me, and noticed that I was quiet and asked what was wrong. I told him that I was trying to figure out how I was going to find a place to live because Rose was moving out and giving up her apartment. We went to the Chinese restaurant across the street and talked. He told me not to worry, he would think of something.

By this time, the weather was changing and it started to get cold. The little money that I did have had to go to my mother and it left me struggling. I didn't have many clothes and Marshall noticed. One evening he came to get me and told me he wanted me to meet someone. He took me to meet his mother. We instantly liked each other. She treated me with so much kindness. Before we left, she went into a room and came back with a winter coat and gave it to me.

"Blessed is he that considereth the poor: the Lord will deliver him in time of trouble" (Psalm 41:1).

After meeting this lady for the first time, I fell in love with her. I met her husband and some of her children. Everyone called Marshall "Poochie." We saw each other every day. He took me to meet his aunts, Thelma and

Elizabeth. Everyone called Elizabeth "Sis." I felt so at home when I was around his family. His brothers and sisters treated me very well because they saw that Poochie was happy and cared very much for me.

During our earlier conversations, I told Poochie about my children, and I told him that I was going home to see my children and invited him to go with me. We went home and he instantly fell in love with my children, especially Lori. He told his aunt Sis about my children and expressed that he wanted me go home and bring my children to Washington. So I went home and brought Gregg and Lori with me. We all lived at his aunt Sis's house with her family. A little later I went and got Juan.

My mother wanted to keep Floyd until school was out before I took him home with me. Sis had a friend who owned houses and rented them out. She told me to apply for public assistance and I spent a whole day in the welfare office applying for it. By the time I was approved, Sis's friend had a house for my children and me. I went home and got Floyd and brought him back with us.

It was summer and everyone was out of school, and it gave me time to make arrangements for my children to enroll in a new school. I moved into the house and rented the entire first floor. This house was located on 1st and Rhode Island Avenue, NE. The rooms upstairs were rented out to a couple of men. They were really nice guys and gave me no trouble. Sis's friend had checked them out and reassured me that they were harmless. Before he moved them in, they came over with him and we talked. The house had two entrances and they did not have to come into my area.

They had an entrance to go directly upstairs. They worked construction, and we made a deal that when I cooked, I would prepare food for them and they would pay me.

Poochie came by almost every day to see us, as he was still living with his aunt Sis. I cared very much for him, mostly out of gratitude. He knew that Herbert was Lori's father. He knew Herbert well. They both hung out around the same spots, M Street, NW. That was the hangout for gamblers and hustlers. One night on my way home to see Mama, we went by this place and saw Herbert. Poochie told me to take Lori in for him to see her. Of course Herbert was polite, but he didn't have much to say. I told him that this was his daughter. He stood there looking stupid, smiling, but he didn't respond. I went back to the car and told Poochie about how he acted. Poochie told me not to worry because Lori belonged to him anyway.

I really was not in love with Poochie, but I cared for him because he loved me. It was rare for me to feel real love from a man. Most of them wanted to have sex, but a committed relationship was not something I felt from most of them. Some of the times Poochie would come over to see me, I noticed that he would be acting funny. He didn't like the fact that men were living upstairs, and one day he moved in upstairs also. I really didn't mind that he moved there. As a matter of fact, I was happy and felt safe knowing he was there. About two months later, my youngest sister, Ree, moved in with me and helped me with the children. By that time, she also was pregnant.

One day Poochie came in and one of the men was in the kitchen where I was fixing his plate. Poochie got angry and started to accuse me of being too friendly with him. I tried to tell him that this man was attracted to my sister Ree. When he realized this was true, he acted better, but I was upset that he was trying to run my life by telling me who my friends could be. We had our arguments, but we continued to stay together.

Another thing that bothered me was the way the man that I rented from would drop in anytime he felt like it. I didn't like that. I was paying my rent on time. I kept the place clean so I didn't feel that he had to always be stopping in, and I expressed that to him. He got an attitude and told me to find another place to live. So here I was once again wondering what I was going to do.

"Give ear to my prayer, O God; and hide not thyself from my supplication" (Psalm 55:1).

By that time Linny and Elijah were living in a house not too far from where I was staying. I stopped by her house one day and told her about what was going on. She went across the street and talked with this man who had a corner store, and he told me that we could rent the upper part of his store. We just had to come through the back way. We really didn't have a choice, so Poochie, my four children, and I moved in. In the meantime, Poochie was out looking for another place to live because there were mice running up and down up there, and they were terrifying my children. A couple of months later, he found a place SE and we moved to Savannah Street across from Saint Elizabeth Hospital.

Poochie and I discussed marriage. He wanted to marry me, and I knew that he was in love with me. I agreed because I felt that he would be the only one who would marry me because I had four children. Folks would say, "She has a ready-made family."

I know that is no reason to marry anyone, but that was the way I felt at the time. So we went home one weekend and got married. My brother Leroy went with us to the pastor's house and we got married out in the yard. It was during the month of June and it was hot. Water was running off of Poochie's face so much that I didn't know if it was because of the heat or he was just that nervous. After we got married, we went to another couple's wedding that same day and celebrated with them.

When Poochie and I were just going together, he was cool with me going out alone and doing my own thing. However, after we got married, all I could hear him say was, "My, my, my. You are my wife; this is my house." And things got ugly quick. He would go out and gamble, come home broke, and try to take it out on me by arguing and eventually fighting me.

He didn't believe in working, but I did. I started to go to school and I learned how to type. I eventually got a job in the government. All my children, except Lori, were in school and everything was going fine.

It seemed as though the more things were working out for me, the angrier Poochie became. He would gamble, get into fights, and then come home and take his anger out on me. After almost two years of that, I got very tired. I never understood men who claimed to love you so much and yet treated you like dirt. I could never wrap my head around that, other than to think that they just didn't like women. I looked for a place to move my children to.

On April 4, 1968, Lori had turned three years old, and I was planning to have a birthday party for her. Later that night, we noticed a fire across the street from where we lived, then another and another.

Looking out the window, we saw folks breaking into the liquor store and the cleaners and taking everything they could. Trucks were pulling up and men were going into the liquor store. They were coming out with cases of liquor and beer. By the time things had quieted down and I got enough nerve, my neighbor and I went over and got a few bottles of wine. We later learned that Dr. Martin Luther King had gotten killed and folks started to riot. It was such a terrible time. We had to be in the house by a certain time because everyone had a curfew. White folks were scared out of their minds because black folks were taking their frustrations out on them. They had to put signs in their car windows as they drove through town saying "Soul sister, Soul brother" to keep from getting attacked.

I had been looking for a place to move to, so shortly after the riots, I found a place in the projects located at 1430 L Street, SE. The next week

I told Poochie that I was leaving and I wanted him to help me move. I rented a truck and moved out. The thing that really made up my mind to hurry up and get out of there was the night he came home with a tooth knocked out because he had been in a fight. I was in bed and he knew what to do to start a fight. He turned on the radio and turned it up loud. I knew he was looking for a fight, so I endured it as long as I could. We lived in the lower level of an apartment, and I knew he was also disturbing our neighbors. So I got up and went into the living room and said, "Poochie, turn that music down. You know you are waking up the neighbors." That was all he needed. He started fussing loudly.

Floyd came downstairs because he was so loud. He looked around and saw Floyd standing there and said, "You better get back up those stairs before I knock you back up there." I will never forget the look on my son's face, and I said to myself, *I am out of here.* I got into bed and left Poochie in the living room listening to the loud music. Later he turned it off and went to sleep in a chair.

"Save me, O God, by thy name, and judge me by thy strength" (Psalm 54:1).

A lot of folks didn't believe me when I told them that I had no idea that Poochie was using drugs. I knew he smoked a little marijuana, but I had no idea that he was shooting heroin. The next day I told him that I was leaving and what I was taking. I left him the bed, some dishes, a chair, and some other things that I knew he would need. I only took things that the children would need. I knew that I would buy things later that I needed to survive. I had to sleep on the floor for a few weeks, but I didn't mind because I had peace in my life at last.

(Angels watching over us!)

I would put the children to sleep and lie on some blankets. I would cry and pray. I thanked God for being with me and giving me peace. I had a lot of work to do. Getting the children in school and going to work to keep food on the table and a roof over our heads was not easy, but I always felt that God was with me.

At that time, I was working for the Department of Human Services and my supervisor was a kind white man who smiled a lot and was very compassionate and considerate. I told him about my situation. After all, we were working at the welfare building. He made some calls and I was able to get twin beds for my children and one full-size bed for myself. That was a blessing.

One day I received a notice that I was going to be evicted from my apartment in the projects. I was working as a grade GS-3 and not making a lot of money. I was trying to do all that I could with the little that I had supporting four small children and myself. I fell behind in paying my rent. I just didn't know what to do. The Bible tells us to train up a child in the way that he should go, and when he grows up, he will not depart from the training. I remembered to call on the name of Jesus when I didn't know anything else to do, so I did just that! I went to my supervisor and told him what I was experiencing. He told me that he would make some calls and not to worry.

The morning the eviction was supposed to happen, I stayed home. I received a call from my supervisor telling me that I would not be evicted because he had taken care of the situation and would see me in the morning when I returned to work. When I came in the next day, he said good morning and went back to work. He never mentioned it again nor did I.

Another reason I knew that God was with me at times was when I would run out of food and really didn't know how or where I would get more. There was a little corner store down the street from where I lived and I would go in sometimes. A man by the name of Alton, we called him Al, ran the place. Al was very kind and we would always talk when I went in. I told him that I needed food but I didn't have any money. He told me to pick out what I needed and he would pay for it. I got enough food to last me until my next payday. He didn't want anything from me other than to be my friend. I loved and respected Al for that, and we remained friends until he died. By this time I was working as a clerk typist at Fort McNair.

"In God have I put my trust: I will not be afraid what man can do unto me" (Psalm 56:11).

I met this man named Larry. He was a good-looking, older man. Each time I would need to Xerox some work he did it for me. He asked me to lunch a few times. And later we start seeing each other. Larry and I had a relationship that lasted about two years before I decided to stop seeing him. He drank a lot, and some of those times he was demanding and controlling of my time, and I didn't like it. Even though Poochie and I were separated at this time, I was not going to have another man telling me what I could and could not do.

One day Poochie knocked on my door and asked if he could stay with me for a couple of weeks until he could find a place. He left the apartment that we had together, and he had moved back into his mother's house. He and his mother had an argument and she told him that he had to leave. I agreed and he stayed for two months.

One day he came in and wanted to start a fight with me. During the time he was at my place, I continued to go out whenever I felt like it. My niece was staying with me and she would be there with the children. He told me that he was not going to stand for me going out. I was his wife and he could still tell me what to do. We got into a big argument and I had to call the police. Two policemen came over and one of them asked me if his name was on my lease. I told him no. This big, tall policeman told him to leave and not come back. He told Poochie, "I am going to check on her, and if you come back here, I am going to come back and kick your ass." Poochie left and didn't come back.

I lived in that project at 1430 L Street, SE for a year and a half. I met a couple of guys whom I dated, but none of them lasted too long. During that time I met a girl by the name of Brenda and we became close. I told her that I was tired of living there because I was having problems with my neighbors.

Four of us lived on the third floor in a section that was in the corner of the building. When I put the children to bed at night, they would all come out of their apartments into the hallway and talk loudly with each other. I heard one of them say, "She thinks she's cute not associating with nobody." Another would say, "Yes, she stays over there like she's better than we are." I would be lying on the floor crying. I knew that I was not the kind of person they made me out to be. When I left my apartment, I would speak and keep on going. I had a job to go to, they didn't. One of the families had a daughter, and one day she wrote on the wall by my door: "MS Brown is a bitch." Many years later, my son Floyd told me that that same girl I had paid to watch them at times would sexually molest them. I asked him why he didn't tell me about it. He said that they knew I had to work and didn't want me to worry about them. I was so hurt to hear that!

I was so ready to leave that place. The lady who lived directly across the hall from me was a fairly nice person. She and I started to talk with one another. She was cool people and we became close, at least to the point where we could hold a conversation. She was a big, tall lady who everyone called Ms. Annabelle.

One night a man climbed up to my balcony. I saw him and started to scream. I opened my door and knocked on Ms. Annabelle's door. I told her that a man was on my balcony. She got a baseball bat, opened my balcony door, and said, "Come on out here, sucker!" He came through and told her that he was trying to get on the fourth floor where his girlfriend lived. She held up that bat and told him to get stepping. I was glad that she was my friend that night.

I really wanted to move out of there. All I was trying to do was go to work and take care of my children and my responsibilities. I knew that I wanted a better life for us, and I was going to do all that I could to make that happen.

One night Brenda, four other women, and I went out to a little club on H Street, NE, and had a few drinks. Later we all left feeling no pain and were being very loud walking to our car. This police vehicle came down the street with two policemen in it. They were very friendly, and one of them actually made a pass at me. He asked me for my phone number and I gave it to him. He called me once, but we never got a chance to get together.

Brenda had bought a home on 4th Street, SE and told me that I could do the same thing. She gave me a number to call and told me that the government would help me to get a house under the Federal Housing Authority (FHA). I called the number and a couple of days later I received a call telling me that someone would come by and take me to look at some houses. For the next two weeks, I went looking at houses. I finally saw a house that I fell in love with. The house was at 1411 19th Street, SE, Washington, DC—the house that I am still in forty some years later.

(Angels watching over us!)

"Blessed is he whose transgression is forgiven, whose sin is covered" (Psalm 32:1).

Poochie never lived there with us, and we never attempted to be together as man and wife again. In December of 1969, I moved into my home on 19th Street. A couple of weeks before I moved in, I went to a party and Herbert was there. We talked and he brought me home that night. I told him that I needed to move, but didn't have anyone to help me. He was driving a van and told me that he would come by and help me move and he did.

I immediately loved our home. It had two bedrooms, a full basement, a nice backyard, and was located on a nice, quiet street. The looks on my children's faces were looks of pure joy. They walked around the house, out in the yard, and up the street—just so grateful to be where they were. Floyd came home one evening and said, "Ma, that man Mr. Al that had ran the grocery store lives up the street in the next block." I went up to see Al and told him that we were living down the street. He told me that he always knew that I would be okay, that I would make it.

I wasn't the only one who went through changes while living in the projects. My children had their share of heartaches also. One of the neighbor's sons tried to put his hands in Lori's panties. She was only four years old but was able to tell me about it, and I went downtown to the police station. Lori told the whole story. He didn't get to actually hurt her, but he tried. Ms. Annabelle had watched Lori for me that day because I had to go to work. The boy was a young boy also, so I don't think anything was actually done to him, but I kept a close eye on my daughter from then on. My boys had to walk to school, and after school a lunch truck would come to the complex and give food out to the children. Ms. Annabelle watched my children until I came in from work.

Now, you would think that I could say that we lived happily ever after by moving into our home. But I can't tell you that I didn't have my share of problems when I moved into our cute little house, because I did. First, the pipes in the basement were old and leaking, and I would wake up with water up to my knees. I lived between two houses. On one side of me was a white lady by the name of Ms. Buckley, on the other side was a black lady by the name of Ms. Mitchell. The water from my basement had flowed into both of their basements. Ms. Buckley told me that Ms. Mitchell called her and asked her if she would go along with her and sue me for damages to their basement. Ms. Buckley told me that she said, "No, I won't do that. The lady has four small children."

The response from the black lady was, "I don't care, and I am going to sue her."

When I heard that, I knew that I had my work cut out for me, and I was getting ready for a battle. Ms. Mitchell was a fairly nice-looking lady and she knew it. She would wear short shorts and halter tops. Her hair was shoulder length and she was soft spoken.

Here I was with four stair-step children, 5 foot 4 ½, and with short-cropped hair. I wasn't ugly, but I never considered myself the dog's bark or the cat's meow, and yet I presented such a threat to this woman. I couldn't understand it. She did everything she could to make my life miserable. I knew that I was going to have problems with this lady, so I sat my children down and explained to them that I wanted them to come straight home from school, stay in the house, and be quiet until I got home from work.

They would get home from school approximately forty-five minutes before I got home. One day I was about to leave my job when I received a call from the Women's Bureau. "Mrs. Brown, we got a call that you left your children home alone, and we are at your house waiting for you."

I rushed home and found a man and a woman in my house. I explained the situation to them and said that I would find someone to watch my children until I returned home. Ms. Mitchell was married, and I heard that her husband was a troubleshooter for then mayor Walter

Washington. This was 1969. They were considered important people in their own eyes and me low class. So they decided to treat me as such.

That wasn't the last time she called the Women's Bureau on me, but the lady at the bureau called me and said, "Mrs. Brown, we got another call from your neighbor and decided that she just doesn't like you. Now, we went to your house again, found your children inside playing with toys and looking at TV. Your refrigerator was full of food, so we decided to leave and not ask you to come home."

There were other times that I would go out, and she would call the bureau on me. After she found that they no longer responded to her calls, she started on her husband to knock on my door and harass me.

One night I was home getting some carpet laid. There was a knock on my door and it was the Mitchells. The missus followed behind her husband. He started by saying, "Mrs. Brown, I have a demanding job, and when I come home, I need to rest. I can't do that because your children are over here throwing balls against the wall and making all kinds of noise. What are you going to do about that?"

I said, "Well, Mr. Mitchell, I am sorry that my children are keeping you from your important sleep by throwing balls they don't have to throw. But I will speak to my children and ask them to stay as quiet as possible." I looked at Mrs. Mitchell standing there with her arms folded and asked her, "What is your problem? You can't hear your soap operas?" By that time, I was good and pissed. I said, "Look, your wife has been giving me the blues ever since I moved here, and I am damn sick and tired of it. I live at 1411 you live at 1413. Take care of where you live and I will do the same where I live. If you feel that I am not good enough to live next door to you, then maybe you should be the ones to move because I am here and here to stay. I am not going anywhere. If your wife intends to sit at her window and call the bureau every time I leave my house, then she had better get a chair and remain there. I am going to leave this house whenever I feel like it, and there is not a damn thing she can do about it." I meant every word I said that day. I'd had enough! They turned on their heels and left, and that was the end of that.

She didn't stop there, but I continued with my life. I met her brother-in-law and found him to be a very nice person. He saw me working in the yard one day when he came to visit his brother. We talked. He said, "I don't find you to be the bitch that I was told you were." We both laughed, and each time he visited he would stop and talk with me. Later that year, I heard that he and his brother succumbed to a horrible death. They were both shot in the head. Drugs were supposed to have been involved. They had two daughters that she would not allow to play with my daughter. I just felt sorry for her and summed it up to her not really having a happy life.

"Hear my voice, Oh God, in my prayer: preserve my life from fear of the enemy" (Psalm 64:1).

At that time, my son Floyd was around eleven years old. He started to get rebellious. I had to resign from my government job at the Department of Human Resources and go on welfare because he was running wild and doing everything that he could. His father kept promising him that he would pick him up, but I would get Floyd ready and his father would never show up.

Floyd started to get into trouble with the law and was in and out of jail at a young age. One evening one of the boys who lived in the neighborhood came to the house and told me that a car had hit Juan. At the time this happened, a friend by the name of Earl stopped by my house. He took me up to the intersection where Juan had gotten hit, and I was told that he had been taken to the hospital. A lady said that she hit Juan. She stated that he was not at the intersection and had run across the street in front of her car. When we went to the hospital, the doctor came out and said that Juan would be okay, but his leg was broken. Juan wanted to follow Floyd everywhere he went and that evening they had broken into a school. Floyd and his friend were also going into houses and stealing. If it wasn't one thing, it was another. During the 1970s, I caught hell with Floyd and he got locked up several times for stealing.

After he returned home, he stopped going to school. Shortly after he quit school, Juan started to get into trouble also. They both stopped going to school, so I took them to Job Corp and enrolled them so they could learn a trade. Floyd took up cement finishing and Juan took up painting.

One evening one of their friends came to the house and told me that Floyd and Juan were involved in a car accident and the car had turned over. Here I go again! By the time I got to the hospital, they had been seen and treated by a doctor. They weren't badly hurt. Juan had a cut on his forehead, and Floyd was just a little shaken up. Shortly after that, they came home from Job Corp.

"God be merciful unto us, and bless us; and cause his face to shine upon us; selah" (Psalm 67:1).

I never liked being on public assistance. I always felt that it was only there to help me out until I could get back on my feet and not for a lifetime. So I would take any jobs that I could get. I worked at a club on 9th Street, NW. During that time, I was introduced to a guy named Warren and went out with him for a while. I also started to work in a trophy shop. I took on any job that I could get to make ends meet. I went for an interview for a Metro Bus Driver, took the test, and got the job. That was in the late 1970s.

One night, Warren was heading to my house when the police stopped him and found drugs on him. They locked him up. He called and asked if I would come downtown to bail him out. While I was waiting for him to come out, who should come in but Billy, the policeman I had met years ago. We remembered each other and again we exchanged numbers. About one week later, he called and we made plans to see each other. Warren and I weren't exclusive anyway. He was married, but he and his wife were separated at the time.

I still didn't like the idea of dealing with married men, so the separation was not hard for me. One day I told him to reconcile with his wife because I was tired of living that type of life. Billy and I began to call each other, but I wasn't ready for another relationship, so I didn't see him for a while. My hands were full dealing with my family situations.

About three months later, Billy called me again and that is when we started a relationship that lasted for several years until the early 1980s. Our relationship was rocky to say the least. As I stated earlier, he was a policeman, and he got around. He felt that he could get just about any woman he wanted, and he tried to do just that.

My next big experience with a job was driving for Metro. It was a big ego booster. I felt that if they trained me, I could learn, and did I learn. I drove that bus better than I could drive a car. It was a great experience that gave me the confidence that I could do anything I made up my mind to do. However, it also had its ups and downs. When I got the job, I didn't own a car. I had to depend on one of my coworkers to pick me up and bring me home. Although we met for the first time in training, he was a good person and he didn't mind picking me up. After being on the job and getting a little money saved, I bought a car. It was such a good feeling. This wasn't my first car. Warren had bought me an old Ford that ran real good for a while, but it started to give me problems just before I got the job driving the bus, so I had to let it go.

The problem with the job of driving the bus was I had to leave home early in the morning and come home late in the evening. That was not good while trying to raise young children.

It was a struggle. I was already having big problems with Floyd acting up, and going in and out of jail and the receiving home for boys. I was trying to hold down a job to support the rest of us. It was a challenge.

I knew that there had to be someone greater than me that was holding us together. I just didn't put it all together at the time. When I got the job driving the bus, they sent me to the Arlington, Virginia, division. When I got there, I found that I was the only woman driver there at that time. I had never been around so many men at one time in my life. I really didn't have time to concern myself with any kind of affair. Billy and I were doing all right, and just learning the routes kept my mind on what I was doing. Just trying to keep my children together was enough for me to deal with.

It was fascinating meeting the guys, both black and white. Yes, a few of the white guys tried to hit on me! But I was cool, and laughed and talked with all of them. One of the older white men came to me and said that he noticed how I interacted with the guys, both black and white. He asked if I would be interested in writing newspaper articles on them for the division. He said that he had that job for a long time and was ready to give it up. All I had to do was pick someone at random and interview them. I took the job and had a ball with it. A lot of the guys were excited that I would choose them to be interviewed. I would ask questions about their family lives, how many children they had, what were their favorite activities, etc. After I gathered all the information, I would take it to the main office at the end of the week and turn it in. The next week, we would get the Metro newspaper and they would read about themselves. That was so much fun for us all.

There was one particular guy there who I could not help but notice. He was the neatest man I had ever seen, and so handsome. He didn't have much to say, but was very friendly. When he smiled, he had a little gap between his front teeth that made him blush when he smiled. When he was not driving, like many of the guys he would sit in the garage and play cards. They would sit around and wait for us rookies, as they called us, and let us catch the jobs that they were supposed to have. They had what you called a pass. If they wanted to, they would pass on a route they didn't want, and the rookies had to take it while they stayed in the garage and played cards. I got caught once or twice and didn't like it at all. One day I went up to this fine hunk of a man and asked if I could interview him for the Metro paper. I sort of flirted with him while asking him questions. I said, "Well, well, what's your name?"

He smiled and said, "Tommy. My name is Tommy."

I said, "Tommy, what's your sign?" At that time, I was heavily into astrology.

He said, "What do you mean?"

I said, "What month were you born?"

He said, "I was born in February."

I got excited and said, "So was I!"

Well, that was the beginning of something great. Tommy and I became good friends with benefits.

He was calm on the job, but wild when he wasn't working. He was what they called a Shop Steward and made decisions as far as the job was concerned. Tommy was very intelligent and very well respected. When he was off the job, he liked to party, drink, and have a good time, and we had a lot of fun together. He and I were so much alike. I think that is why we got along so well.

It wasn't long after my training days were over that the company went on strike. I was told that I didn't have to participate and march because I was just coming on board. I did go to a meeting one night and the drivers won the strike.

Most of the guys and girls on the job came over to my house and we partied all night. My children were accustomed to parties because I had them often. They would take folks' coats and put them away for them, but by the time the party was over, my children would all be upstairs asleep.

The relationship between Billy and me was not going very well. I found out that he was seeing an older woman about two blocks up the street from me, and that didn't sit well with me at all. One day I saw him driving her car. He was a lady's man, and I was getting fed up with the whole idea of being his part-time fling. I didn't feel guilty about seeing other people, since he was doing the same thing. Our relationship was stormy at best. We knew we were both in trouble, but we held on for some reason. It reminded me of the song that Gladys Knight sang: "Neither one of us wants to be the first to say good-bye." We held on to each other knowing that it was just a matter of time before it came to an end. Tommy was handsome, sweet, and fun to be with, but he was also married. He and his wife were separated and had been for a while. He was lonely, and I found out that was why he drank so much. His wife was ill and she later died.

I drove the bus for eighteen months and got fired because I had three accidents. It was easy for them to fire you before your probation period was over. I almost made it, but I slid on some ice and ran into another bus that was full of people. Luck had it that no one was hurt, so I dodge that bullet. After I left the bus company, I got a job working at a nightclub, which was a totally different experience.

I felt like a little girl leaving the country again. I really wasn't accustomed to the nightlife, such as clubs and the things that took place in clubs, especially the clubs on 14th Street, NW. I started working on 9th Street and ended up working for a guy named Chuck. He owned a club on 14th Street.

I worked during the day, so I didn't really know what nightlife at Chuck's was like. One day, one of the girls that worked at night asked me if I would work in her place and she would work during the day for me. I agreed and came to work around 5:00 that evening. Things were going fine—the music was loud and the gay men were out in full force. I went back into the kitchen and heard this song playing. I came back in and saw this pretty young girl on the stage dancing. My mouth flew open and I couldn't shut it. Chuck came over and asked me what was wrong. I said, "That girl doesn't have any clothes on."

He started to laugh and said, "You've never seen anybody with their clothes off?"

I said, "No, not on stage dancing where everyone is looking at her."

The guys were not only looking at her, but one guy was sitting right at the stage looking up at her and touching her. I felt sick to my stomach. I went back into the kitchen and sat down. When the dance was over, she came back in the kitchen naked, walking like there was nothing to it. She went into the refrigerator and got a bottle of water. I asked her, "How old are you?" She said, "Sixteen." My heart broke for her. I asked if she had a boyfriend and what he thought of her dancing naked. She told me that he was out there and was her manager. I soon got tired of that kind of life and felt that I had to spend more time at home with my children. It was 1979, all my children were at home, and things were going pretty well.

"Save me, O God, for the floodwaters are up to my neck. Deeper and deeper I sink into the mire" (Psalm 69:1).

I decided that I would try to get a government job again. That was the main reason why I came to Washington, DC, in the first place. I went down to the General Service Administration (GSA) building and saw that they were hiring folks in temporary positions. I applied for a clerk typist position and got the job. I have to say that every job that I applied for, I got.

(Angel watching over me!)

I started work and boy did they have work for me to do. I didn't mind working hard, as I was so grateful to be working in a decent, respectable job. After three weeks, my supervisor asked me if I would like to work full time and I said, "Yes, sir." He told me that he was putting my papers in for a full-time position. I said, "Thank you very much, sir!" I was again working for the federal government.

I met some cool people while working at GSA. Billy would pick me up some evenings, sometimes by car, sometimes by motorcycle. We were still holding things together, trying to make it work.

The job wasn't hard, just a lot of typing. My grade was a GS-3 Clerk Typist, and I wasn't making much money. I needed to make more, so I went into the employment office again and started looking for a position with a higher grade. I read that the Federal Protective Service was hiring for a head GS-5 Clerk Typist position. I applied for that job, and after my initial interview I got it. After I received the papers that I was hired, my present supervisor acted like he didn't want me to go. He asked if I could stay on for a while longer and teach a new girl my job. The new girl was hired as a GS-5 in the same position that I was working as a GS-3, and I was expected to teach her the job. I called Chief Linwood Hardmon and asked him to tell these people to let me go, and the following week I was gone.

I knew when I walked into the office I would enjoy working there. I was working with retired servicemen. My supervisor was a retired lieutenant colonel. Also in the office were Capt. Calvin Taylor, Lt. James Belt, Lt. Webb Mitchell, Lt. Ray Pyle, and later Lt. John Poston. I felt comfortable working with these men. They treated me very well. My boss, Chief Hardmon, was a good man, but I later found out that he was an alcoholic. This did not interfere with his job, as he was a very intelligent man.

I started work in October 1980. I was the lead secretary, and later a girl by the name of Reitta was hired to work for Lt. James Belt, then a girl by the name of Alva was hired to work for Capt. Calvin Taylor. Later Pearl Jackson came on board.

Capt. Poston was a tall, handsome guy and immediately had eyes for me. He came from the Pentagon to work with us. He was a laid-back sort of guy who would pull up a chair and talk to me as I did my work. This did not go very well with Chief Hardmon, and he didn't really care who knew it. I guess the chief knew the captain's reputation, because later I would find out that he was a womanizer and practically had a girlfriend at every office he worked in. We dated for a while, but again I found out that he was married. One evening he brought me home and Billy was at my house waiting for me.

When he saw me getting out of the captain's car, Billy ask me if the captain was taking his place. I told him no there was nothing to it, as he just gave me a ride home. Although he was very kind, I truly did not want another married man in my life. I was looking for a way out, and got it when he was sent away on his job for a few months. While he was away, he got involved with a lady at work and I found out. That was really the end of our fleeting affair.

Before he left, he took me to the Pentagon and introduced me to a guy by the name of Henry Gater. He told Henry to take care of me while he was gone, and Henry was more than glad to do so. After a few weeks, Henry and I started to see each other.

When the captain came back, I confronted him and told him that everyone at work had heard about him and the lady who he was involved with. He started to really fall for this lady, but she did what he was accustomed to doing—she broke his heart and made a fool out of him.

When he returned, he found out that Henry and I were seeing each other and he didn't like it one bit, but there was nothing he could do about it. After all, he was a married man and Henry was not. Although he knew that Henry was picking me up from work every evening, he still tried to have a relationship with me. Chief Hardmon saw what was going on, and it wasn't long before the good captain was back at the Pentagon.

Everyone thought the colonel and I had something going on, including his wife. That was not true. The colonel and I never crossed the line. We just got along very well. One day his wife came to the job to see him and walked right past my desk into his office. That was the first time I saw and spoke to her. She didn't say anything back, but continued into his office. The next day, I told the chief that his wife walked right past me and didn't acknowledge me. He laughed and told me that she accused him of liking me. Everyone told me that the chief liked me, but I knew that nothing was going to happen between us, and nothing ever did.

My father passed away the following year, and I was allowed to take off for a week. Ten years later in 1991, my mother passed away. One day while visiting my mother, she asked me if I lived in Baltimore. I told her no, I lived in Washington, DC. About five minutes later, she asked me the same question and I responded the same. About three minutes later, she ask me the question again. I stopped and looked at her and my heart sank. That was when I realized that my dear mother was suffering from Alzheimer's.

"Oh Lord God of my salvation, I have cried day and night before thee" (Psalm 88:1).

My heart just broke and I cried all the way back to Washington, DC. I had to stop my car a couple of times because I could not stop crying. I could only think of this strong lady I had known all my life now suffering from something that would limit her activities. All my mother's siblings had passed away before she did at the age of eighty-one.

I had noticed her staring into space as if she didn't know what was going on at her sister's and brother's funeral. I felt so sad for her. She seemed so helpless. She would forget a lot of things, but when my son Floyd walked into the house, she would say, "Hi Floyd!" She had the biggest smile on her face when she saw him. She never forgot Floyd. Shortly after she passed, I was lying in bed with my back turned to my bedroom door. I felt this presence approach the doorway. I really can't describe it, but to say it was someone or something standing in the doorway. I tried to move, to turn over, but I could not move. After a few moments, it left and I was able to turn over. After a few days, it happened again. This time, I had the mind to speak to it. I said, "Mama, I know that it's you. I'm all right, Mama. Everything is okay and you can go in peace now." It left and never returned. I know without a doubt that it was my mother's spirit coming back to see if we were okay and to let me know that she was watching over us. I will never forget that as long as I live. I felt so peaceful after that.

My children were growing up now, and we didn't have any problems at that time. Floyd had bought himself a big, old station wagon. The day before my father was buried he was working on it and had parts all over the place. I asked him if he would be able to put the parts back together again and bring his brothers and sister down to the funeral.

He said that he would. In the back of my mind, I didn't think that he could, but the next day he was pulling up with Juan, Gregg, and Lori. I was so proud of him because he had come a long way. He, along with a friend and neighbor named Brian, put that station wagon back together and drove it all the way to Maryland to my father's funeral.

One day I was at work and the phone rang. On the other line was someone calling me from the Montgomery County Police Department telling me that my son Floyd and three other guys were locked up for robbing a bank. I started to scream, and the chief came in and took the phone and spoke to the person on the other end. Capt. Taylor took me home and the next day he took me to the courthouse. To this day, I don't know what involvement they had in this matter, but these retired servicemen did something. The judge released Floyd the following day. She told him that he had friends in high places and she never wanted to see him in her courtroom again. She reminded him that he was about to turn eighteen years of age, and if he committed another crime, he would be charged as an adult. Floyd never went back to Montgomery County again or had to go to court. As a matter of fact, that was the last time my son got into any trouble with the law.

I talked with Floyd and asked him what in the world was he thinking to rob a bank. He told me he and three other boys, one named Major Quarles who lived a block up from us, decided that Floyd had the right car, that old station wagon, to go and rob this bank. I had seen them standing on the corner the night before talking, but I had no idea that this is what they were planning to do.

They went in this bank to try to take this machine out, but could not get it, so they left. Shortly afterward, they realized that they had left their tools there so they went back to get them and ran into a number of Montgomery County policemen. They jumped out of the car and tried to run, but the police had dogs. Floyd said that he just stopped and put his hands up so the dogs wouldn't get him. Another fellow ran but was almost eaten up by the dogs. I saw that guy in court and he didn't look too good. He was bandaged up from dog bites. No one at my job ever spoke of this incident again. Floyd went to church, got baptized, and didn't get into any more trouble with the law. He finally realized that he was given a chance of a lifetime to have dodged that bullet. I don't know what happened, but I knew that it had to be divine intervention into our lives once again!

(Angels watching over us!)

> *"I will sing of the mercies of the Lord forever: with my mouth will I make known thy faithfulness to all generations" (Psalm 89:1).*

Henry and I spent a lot of time together going out to clubs and shows. We had a lot of fun together. He made me laugh a lot and my children liked him. He was very protective of me and treated me very well. He would even drop me off to spend time with my friends and then pick me up.

Lori came to me one day and said, "I've got some good news and some bad news." I told her to tell me the good news first. She said, "Well, I am pregnant."

I said, "What is the bad news?"

"I won't be going to school anymore."

Lori never liked going to school and I felt sad for her because I saw her going down the same road that I did. But like my mother, I didn't scold her. I just told her that I would be there for her.

The night she went into labor, I was at Henry's apartment. Gregg called and told me that Lori was ready to have her baby. Henry and I jumped into his little 280Z and rushed home. We picked Lori up and headed to the hospital. Tamia was born on December 31, 1982, New Year's Eve. Henry instantly fell in love with her. He watched over Lori and Tamia like a hawk. Tamia didn't want for anything because he made it his business to get her everything she needed. He really loved that little girl.

Our relationship was going well for a long time and we decided to live together. Henry liked to drink and have fun, but after a time, I started to notice that he was going out and not inviting me to go along with him. There were times when we would go to this lady and her husband's house to visit and have a few drinks. One night he went out and didn't come home. The next morning he came in and stated he had gotten drunk, pulled over to the side of the road, and went to sleep. Several times he would stay out late, and when he came in, he had some stupid excuse. He didn't realize that I never believed any of the lies he was telling me.

One morning before I went to work, I told him to look for another place to live because we were merely living together and not married or obligated to each other. I was not going to be disrespected. I told him if he had someone out there that he wanted to spend time with, by all means go with them, but not while he was living with me. He found an apartment in the same complex where he once lived.

He continued to come over and see me. Our relationship was still intact and we continued to go out on dates, and he eventually moved back into my house.

One day I borrowed his car to go to the country to visit my folks. I noticed a piece of white substance on the floor of the car and found out that it was crack. When I came home and confronted him with it, he told me that he had some friends in the car and one probably left it. I knew that I was not going to deal with that from him. Here was this grown man, a policeman who had many years in the federal government, acting so irresponsible with his life and mine. I told him that he had to go. He soon moved out and got his own place once again.

I was so happy the day that my son Gregg got married. We went to his wedding and celebrated all day long. When I came home that evening, I found my door opened and my closet and Lori's closet almost cleaned out. Later we found out that my son Juan had stolen the clothes to pay for crack. My life changed that day and was a total nightmare for a very long time after that.

I have been hurt many times—some by affairs gone bad, some by betrayal of friendships that I've put faith and time into—but I have never felt the hurt and pain that I experienced when my son got hooked on crack. He started out selling drugs. He got robbed several times, even shot, and he made it through those awful times. Soon he started to use his product and got hooked.

I had to lock him out of my home. At least I thought I had locked him out. He managed to get in every time I left home. It was as if he was watching me to see when I left, then he would come in and steal everything that wasn't locked down. There were times I would wake up and feel this cold air.

I would go downstairs and find my door and windows open. Juan would come through the window, take whatever he could, and leave through the back door, leaving it open while I was upstairs in bed asleep. He took just about all the gifts from under the Christmas tree that Lori would buy for Tamia when she was a baby. His only mind-set was to take anything he could sell. During the Christmas holidays, I decided to buy him some shoes because the shoes he was wearing were ragged with holes in them. His gift was the first that I bought, along with twelve pairs of socks. I gave those things to him a little before Christmas. When I saw him later, he had on the same ragged shoes. I asked him where the shoes and socks were that I had bought him and he told me he had to sell them.

I was so hurt because I knew that he was really in trouble. It tore my heart apart to see him in that condition. I even saw some of my things in a neighbor's house one day when I visited. I made a promise to myself that I would never buy anything that anyone tried to sell to me on the street. They were most likely stolen from someone.

I have never cried so much in my entire life. Not even when I was getting beat up by Peter or my husband. Finally, one night after about a full year of him living on the streets, looking bad, and smelling worse, I fell on my knees and prayed to God to help me. I cried, "Lord, I don't know what to do. Please help me!" I was scared to look at the news, fearing I would see or hear that he was dead. Whenever I heard a siren, I would run to the window and look out, hoping that the phone wouldn't ring with someone telling me that my son was hurt or dead.

When you cry out to God, you'd better be ready for an answer, and I got an answer from Him. When you hear that God works in mysterious ways, you can believe it. I cried out to Him and He answered by telling me what to do and how to do it.

I found myself thinking, *What is in here that he hasn't taken yet?* I thought of this little television I kept on the counter that I watched when I was working in the kitchen. I knew that he would soon come back to get that, and surely as I am writing this, he came that same night to get it.

(Angels watching over us!)

I knew there was only one way he could get in and that was through the basement window. I put a lamp under it so I could hear if he came in that way. I turned my bedroom light out and waited. It wasn't long before I heard the lamp crash. This was like a script that was written especially for me. He came upstairs, got the TV, and started out of the front door because he couldn't go through the back. I had a lock on the back door that you needed a key to get out. When he got in the front yard, I hollered out the window, "Bring it back!"

He started to cry, saying, "Mama, I need to take this 'cause I need to get the money so they won't kill me!"

I said, "Son, if someone was going to kill you, you would have been dead by now, so bring my TV back." I went downstairs and told him to sit down. I said, "I'm going to do something tonight to save your life."

I got on the phone and called 9-1-1. I told them that I had someone who had broken into my house, I had them by knifepoint, and to hurry and send someone. At first, I don't think he believed that I was really calling the police. When it occurred to him that I was calling for real, he jumped up and said, "No, Ma, I can't go to jail." He started out the door and that's when I saw police cars coming from every direction.

They jumped out of the cars with guns pointed at my son. They told him to get down on the ground. Juan was so surprised he just stood there. They threatened to shoot him if he didn't get on the ground. I told him to get on the ground before they shot him, so he did. They put my son in the car. I cried and cried so much my eyes and head hurt. One of the black policemen came into the house and asked if I knew him. I said, "Yes, he's my son."

He said, "Your son? How could you call the police on your own son?"

I said, "Officer, don't sit here and chastise me about calling the law on my son. I am saving my son's life before someone like you out there kills him. You have no idea what I've been dealing with for the past year with my son—getting robbed, shot, and being homeless. So don't you dare sit here and try to tell me how to handle this situation. I know what I am doing." He got up and walked out of the house without another word.

I cried and prayed and thanked God for answering my prayers. I slept that night better than I had for a year. I now knew where my son was.

Approximately four months after Juan's arrest, he wrote me a letter and thanked me for having him locked up. He was able to kick his drug habit and think more clearly than he had in a long time.

(Angels watching over us.)

Although he had kicked the habit, Juan's problems weren't over. He had to do four years' back time for violating his parole. When it was time for him to go to court, I wrote the judge a letter and asked that she put my son in a rehabilitation program versus doing four years of jail time. To my surprise and amazement, she wrote me back and told me that she would send him to Durham, North Carolina. I wrote back to the judge and thanked her very much! After two years of jail time, he was able to come home for a couple of days before he had to go away to rehab. After those couple of days at home with me, his lawyer came by and took him away. He spent two years in North Carolina in a rehab facility.

After Juan completed rehab, he came home and immediately got two jobs. He has been working ever since. He went from stealing everything that he could get his hands on to having keys to both churches called Galilee Baptist. Praise the Lord! He stayed with me until he could get on his feet, and bought enough furniture to fill an apartment. He met a woman, fell in love, and moved out.

"I will not forget you. See, I have inscribed you on the palms of my hands" (Isaiah 49:15–16).

I had a couple of love affairs after that ordeal was over, but nothing that lasted. I decided to put my energies into work. I loved my job because it gave me opportunities to do what I enjoyed doing—speaking at seminars and meeting people from all walks of life. I traveled to places I would not have ordinarily had the opportunity to go. I went to Dallas, New Orleans, Florida, and Georgia. In my wildest dreams, I never thought that I would have a job I enjoyed so much.

I was promoted from Clerk Typist GS-5 to Physical Security Specialist GS-12 for the Department of Homeland Security. I was making a good salary and able to have some of the things I always dreamed of having—including nice cars and a comfortable home to live in. My children were all doing well.

I joined a band that was put together on the job by Capt. Leonard Copeland. We were called "The Living Color Band and Show." Members consisted of James Smith, Talmidge Hill, Eunice Gorham, Jasper Gilmore, John Baker, Leonard Copeland, and me. We put our voices and talent together and performed on the Mall, at government facilities, and at company picnics. We also performed at a Blacks in Government (BIG) conference one year.

"I will restore to you the years that the swarming locust has eaten" (Joel 2:25).

Of course there are always haters when some folks feel someone else is having more fun than they are. But the haters were shot down, because our director, Mr. Peter Coles, was pleased with our performance and enjoyed our shows.

We lost one of our band members when James died in 1997, and a part of us died with him. Our last performance was at a retirement ceremony at Boiling Air Force Base. Three of the guys who were band members retired that day, and it wasn't long after that we were separated and that was the end of a wonderful experience. I reminisce every once in a while with photos. What a wonderful experience to look back on and smile about.

I knew that God always watched over me. I thought that some of the things I had been through only God brought me through. There were many relationships that did not last long. Some were abusive and controlling, and some were with men being unfaithful to their wives. I often cried when I thought of how I would get into these relationships knowing they would not last, but I was still always looking for the love of a man. I guess I just missed having the relationship that I craved with my father.

I would see people who seemed liked they had so much love for each other, and I would ask myself, *Why can't I ever have a relationship like that?* They seemed to really love each other, and it was not just a one-sided affair like I always had. I never really felt that any of the men I cared about really cared for me the same way. Other than my husband, I don't think I was loved by any of them. They all lusted for me, but they didn't love me. To this day, I am still friendly with some of the men I once had a relationship with because we never parted hating each other. We are still able to talk and laugh, and even hug, because there is a mutual respect that we still have for one another. I never felt hate for any of them because I was just as much at fault for anything that occurred as they were. I found myself praying for the ones who abused me because their lives didn't end well.

Although I had always gone to church, and grew up in church during those years, I was only going every now and then now. Parties and drinking on a Saturday night kept me in bed most Sunday mornings. I woke up one Sunday morning and this particular Sunday morning I decided to go to church. It was 1982. Reverend Simms, an undershepherd of Pastor Eugene Weathers, was preaching at Galilee South that morning. While listening to him preach the word of God, something got ahold of me and wouldn't let me go. Immediately, I knew it was the Holy Spirit speaking to my heart, and when they opened up the doors to the church, I got up and joined. That day I gave my heart to Christ Jesus, and it was the best day of my life. The first ministry I joined was the Usher Ministry. I also joined the choir and loved singing the gospel of our Lord and Savior, Jesus the Christ, and I loved every minute of it.

There are times when I run into someone who remembers me when I was out there in the world singing and they ask me if I am still singing. I tell them, "Yes, I am still singing, but now I am singing for the Lord and I am still enjoying it."

Although Henry and I weren't still living together, I still cared for him and we remained friends. I later heard that he and this woman that he was creeping with while he was living with me had rented this house. She was not living there, but he was. I saw him walking one day, and I picked him up and carried him home. He said he wanted a pack of cigarettes, but he either had to get something to eat or buy cigarettes.

I didn't have a lot of money with me that day, but I gave him what I had. I went to visit my folks in the country that day. On my way back I stopped by the Safeway store and bought all kinds of food for him. When I dropped the food off, he was a bit embarrassed, but grateful. Later, I learned that they didn't have the gas on, so they couldn't even cook the food. My son told me to stop going by there because the people staying there with him were all was on drugs. I never went back there and later heard that he had moved back home to Alton, Illinois. I was glad to hear that. Once a year he calls me and we laugh and talk. He told me that he was driving a school bus, so I knew that he was no longer using drugs, and I felt real good about that.

One of the things that I am proud of is that most of the men who came into my life I can still laugh with and call them friends. I feel that everyone is not supposed to stay in your life. There are reasons and seasons for everything and everybody. Some folks hate each other when the relationship goes sour, and some want to kill the other. But I never had any hard feelings when my relationships came to an end. I guess I never thought they would last anyway. I thank God that I do not feel that way about any of the men who came into my life and are now gone.

My children were all young when I moved to 1411 19th Street, SE, Washington, DC, and grew up at that address. My house caught on fire twice. The first time, Floyd left a frying pan on the stove on a low burner and forgot and left the house. I was at work at the time, and when I got home, the fire department was there putting out the fire. We had to move out for a while until our home was repaired. The second time, I knocked over a propane tank in the basement into the hot water heater and it exploded. As I was running out the front door, my whole picture window blew out. I had a large plant in that window and it was lying out in the front yard. After the fire was put out, one of the men came across the street where I was sitting. He told me that I was very lucky to have gotten out of the house in time. I told him, "No, sir, luck had nothing to do with it. It was the blessing of God in my life." I believed it then and I still believe it now. I didn't get hurt, but I had to move out for about nine months.

Four months after I moved back in, I had a house blessing and invited my family and friends. My house was packed with just about everyone that I invited. It was a wonderful time to see all of my family there. Juan spoke and there wasn't a dry eye in the house. Rev. Owen Gayles, an associate preacher to our pastor, Rev. Lloyd McGriff, blessed our home.

As I look back over my life and think things over, I do find that my good days surely outweighed my bad days. My son Gregg graduated from high school and went into the army. He served our country for twenty years and now resides with his wife and two sons in Columbia, South Carolina, including two grandchildren. My son Juan has his own place, works every day, and goes to church on a regular basis. He is a fine gentleman with a good heart and a kind spirit and has five children and seven grandchildren. My son Floyd has no biological children. However, he is now married and has stepchildren and grandchildren. He is wonderful to them. If you didn't know it, you couldn't tell that he is not the biological father and grandfather of those children. He is a minister and is preaching the gospel of Jesus Christ, and you can't get any better than that. My daughter Lori is married with a grown daughter, Tamia, who is now married and has a son named Darrell. He calls me GG, short for great-grandma.

"Blessed the Lord my strength, which teacheth my hands to war and my fingers to fight" (Psalm 144:1).

In 2000, I started to buy food to feed single parents. I would see these young women walking with one child in their arms, one tugging at their leg, and one in a walker. I would think of my four small children walking with me to catch a bus or visiting someone. I felt for them and wanted to do something to help. That is when I got the idea to try to give back something because God had been so good to me.

In the beginning, I was buying damaged cans goods and food that the store could no longer sell. I was able to get it at a reduced price. I would save coupons and buy anything I could at a reduced price. One day I was asked to be the chairperson of a share food program for the church. The food packages consisted of meat, vegetables, fruits, and pastries—all nourishing food for twenty dollars. My job was to take orders from folks and have their food ready for them to pick up once a month. This was a wonderful program, but it started to overwhelm me, as there were so many orders. I asked some of the women in church to help me out. For the first two months, I had twelve women helping. The numbers started to dwindle and I ended up with one faithful person helping me to this very day. Her name is Ms. Karen Canada.

During that time, I met Ms. Wilson. She was living in a place for seniors. Ms. Wilson was a hard-working lady, dedicated to what she was doing. She would bring me seven or eight orders at a time from where she was living. We would pack up her car with food and take it to the residence and give it out to those who ordered it. One day as we were talking, she told me that she loved my spirit and asked if I was interested in coming to where they lived and teach Bible study. I had to pray on this request and asked God if this was something he approved of me doing. Two weeks later, I called Ms. Wilson and told her that I would do it. I taught Bible studies on Tuesday nights for the next six years. Ms. Wilson became ill and later she died. Her son called me and asked if I would give the eulogy at her funeral. At first I was reluctant, but after he told me that his mother wanted it that way, I agreed. It was a beautiful homegoing service. We all missed her so much, and I continued to teach.

One evening as I was leaving the residence, I noticed this man giving out food to the people. I introduced myself to him and we began to talk. He said, "I am Deacon Clark Glenn from St. Ignatius Church." We talked about what he was doing. He told me that he had several places where he would get food from and was willing to give up one of those places to let me get food from there. The following week I went to a store located in Accokeek, Maryland. I was told to go to the rear of the store, knock on the door, and tell them that Deacon Glenn sent me. I did and was received by a black woman who looked at me like I smelled bad. Although she was cool toward me for a while, she would let me in, but sometimes keeping me waiting on purpose.

The food they would give me was food that they could no longer sell, so it had to be distributed and consumed fast. I was able to get the food for several weeks. One day the supervisor of the store informed me that they could no longer allow me to have it, as I was not insured with the store. If someone got sick from eating it, they could be held liable. I understood, thanked him, and left. I later called Deacon Glenn and told him what happened. He asked me to meet him the next week at another location.

When I arrived, he was there in the office talking to a gentleman who introduced himself as Mr. Oliver Johnson. It has been twelve years since that introduction and Mr. Johnson is still preparing food packages once a month for me and my son Floyd, who later joined me in this ministry that is named "True Agape Outreach Ministry Connection, Inc." Fourteen years later, my son and I are still getting food from Mr. Johnson's establishment, and we are feeding the needy. God is so good!

(Angels watching over us!)

I feel very blessed. I retired from the government at sixty-five in the year of 2006. After staying home for a while, I decided to go back to school. It was something that had been bothering me for a long, long time.

Even though I was blessed to have successfully worked at jobs that I loved and were fulfilling to me, I still didn't have my high school diploma.

My son Gregg was totally surprised to hear that I had not gotten it. I told him that it was no one but God who had given me opportunities to have a wonderful career and jobs that I really didn't think I deserved. But that's the kind of God we serve.

I went back to school, studied, and passed all my courses. I found myself mentoring other classmates. Most of them were young, single parents who had dropped out of school early and decided to go back to further their education. Our teacher was a nice man named Mr. Hart. He was a very good teacher with patience and took the time to see if we understood what he was teaching us. He did not tolerate excuses of any kind, but he was graceful and understanding of situations and circumstances. He was also a minister and a humble soul. I love him so much for being such an inspiration to me. I found it very easy to talk and confide in him on a personal level. He always had good advice to impart to us all.

I graduated the oldest in my class and received a Lifetime Learners Award. I was a very proud mother, grandmother, and great-grandmother. It felt good knowing that I had achieved the goal I set for myself. I didn't plan to stop there. I went on to enroll in the University of the District of Columbia (UDC), a community college, and my major is communication. I decided to take courses online.

(Angel watching over me.)

I aspire to become a motivational speaker to encourage others to follow their dreams and never give up no matter what age they are. As long as we are breathing and God keeps us in our right minds, we have a chance to achieve our goals. We also need to keep faith in God and a belief in ourselves.

Our Bible tells us not to grow weary in well doing, for in due season we shall reap if we don't faint (don't get discourage or tired). That scripture can be found in the book of Ephesians chapter 6. I won't tell you which verse because I want you to read the entire chapter. It will overwhelm you with blessings for your soul, and I don't want you to miss that!

My ex-husband passed away November 23, 1996, after a long illness. I heard that he was hospitalized.

We had been divorced for a while now. We had been separated for almost twenty-five years when I decided that although we didn't bother each other, I should file for a divorce just in case he or I decided to get married again. After I filed, I received a call from my lawyer who I had hired several months prior, and he asked if I was sitting down. I told him that I was lying down, as it was late at night. He told me that my husband was contesting the divorce. I could not believe it. We had been separated for so long that I didn't think he wouldn't want a divorce. After all, I was planning to pay for it.

The day we went to court, Poochie got up and lied about everything. He told the judge that he lived in the same house that we had moved into. When the judge asked him what year he moved in, he couldn't remember. He started to make up dates and times. Poochie never set his foot in our home. The judge had gotten so frustrated with him that he asked if someone had something for a headache.

After the judge asked a few more questions of my husband and me, the judge granted me an absolute divorce, effective immediately, and ordered the lawyer to return all the money that I had paid him prior. Poochie walked out of the courthouse, and I believe I saw him about three times after that. When we would run into each other, we greeted each other with a hug and a short conversation.

The day I went to the hospital to see him, he told me that I was the last one that he expected to see. I told him that I had no ill feelings toward him, and I started to feed him when the nurse brought his food in. His mother came and finished feeding him. I cried so hard when I left his room that day because I knew he wasn't going to be with us much longer, and he wasn't. He died the next week.

Floyd and Gregg's father, Buddy, died on June 3, 1990, after a long illness. I didn't get to see him before he died. The day Floyd and I went to see him we were told that he had been transferred to another hospital. The next day we heard that he had died. We were told that he asked for Floyd before he died. Floyd was okay because he and his father did get together and spend time with each other after Floyd became a young man. Buddy finally admitted that Gregg and Floyd were his sons and started to call them son.

"Praise waiteth for thee, O God, in Zion: and unto thee shall the vow be performed" (Psalm 65:1).

There was a knock on my door. When I went to answer it, I didn't recognize the man standing there. I asked, "May I help you?" He took off his sunglasses and immediately I knew it was Billy. I hadn't seen him in over twenty-five years. He smiled and I could not believe my eyes. I was telling a friend about two days before that it was so strange that after an affair was over, I never ran into any of my old flames. I never ran into them at the malls, the stores, the church, or on the street. Now here was Billy standing there smiling.

I invited him in and we sat down and talked for about three hours. He showed me pictures of his family. His daughter and his son were both grown up now, and good-looking children. Billy's life had changed as well as mine. We both joined the church and served in several ministries—he, Elder Davis, and me, Deaconess Brown. It was refreshing to visit with him. Neither of us talked about our past and the way we were. We just enjoyed talking about the life we were living now.

I would be lying if I said that some of the old feelings didn't come back. He was on my mind for a few days after he left. I prayed so hard to God to take those thoughts out of my mind. The next evening I opened my mailbox and found a card that he had obviously left that day. It had his name on it. His title was elder. His church address, telephone number, his personal number, and e-mail address were on the card. I spoke to one the ministers at my church about my feelings. I had confidence that what we talked about would stay between us.

Billy had always been a man of integrity and conviction. I knew he cared a lot for me when we were seeing each other, and we had mutual respect for each other. Even though I remembered that he was a womanizer and had his pick of women, he showed me that I was special to him. He was a policeman and women seemed to like men in uniform. His occupation didn't concern me that much, as I felt that I could compete with anyone as far as work was concerned, and I was accustomed to working with men in uniform.

I knew that he wanted a family, and I knew that the woman who had his child would be the one he would marry. He told me that he wanted me to have his child, but during the time he and I were together, I went to the doctor and had an operation that prevented me from having any more children. I really did not want any more. When I found out that he had gotten this woman pregnant, I knew that our relationship was over. As much as it hurt me, I was not going to be someone he snuck around with. I felt that he had made his choice. So the relationship between us was over.

I know that my life has changed. I am not the same gullible and needy person I had been in the past. I do not have low self-esteem—I know what I am worth today.

I am a child of the King, and He has given me something that I am proud of, and that is self-love, dignity, and respect for myself and respect for the woman he married. I don't have to settle anymore. Plus, I read in the book of Ephesians and a few more books in the Bible that fornication, uncleanliness, or covetousness should not be named among me as a child of God.

Billy and I will always be friends because we basically know so much about each other, but that is as far as our relationship will go. I know that the flesh is weak, but I also know that God will keep me strong if I pray to Him and ask Him, and I have asked Him to do just that and I mean it.

I have a picture of Mama and Daddy hanging in my bedroom and sometimes late at night I talk to them. I thank my mother for the kind, loving, and wonderful strong person that she was. I thank her for being such a compassionate and understanding individual.

I think of the times that I had my babies, took them home to her, left them for her to care for, and she did it without complaining a single word. I cry a lot when I think about that. I feel that it was unfair for me to even think that I could do that. But I knew that she loved my babies as much as I did, or even more. I don't know if that is possible, but she had to love them and me to do what she did. I don't know if I could do that with four children. I do know that I didn't mind taking care of my grandchild Tamia. I feel that I had to give back and be as considerate with my daughter as my mother was with me.

Besides, I loved when Tamia was with me because I knew that I was going to take good care of her, and I am still taking care of her. I know that she is married and has a son and a husband, but she calls me every day. I realize that I have other grandchildren, but they are all scattered about and have other grandmothers they are close to. My oldest granddaughter, Juan's daughter Nikita, seldom calls, but I know in her own way she loves me, and I love her very much. I intend to be here for all my children, grandchildren, and great-grands whenever they need me.

Floyd is such an inspiration to me and I thank God for him every day of my life. He decided to go back to school and get his high school diploma before I did. It was going to his graduation and seeing him walk up and get his diploma that made me decide that I would do it also. He introduced me to one of his teachers, and I expressed to her that I wanted to do the same thing. They both encouraged me to do it. I am very proud of Floyd and the way he completely turned his life around. My regret is that his father didn't live long enough or spend more time with his sons to know what wonderful men they became.

I feel sad sometimes when I think of my children and how there has never really been a strong father in their lives, but I know within my heart and soul that God never makes mistakes, and He has been with us all our lives. He is our Father! God made a promise to us that He would never leave or forsake us, and I know that His word is true. I thank God every day for blessing and keeping us through the good times and the not-so-good times.

I have decided to write an account of my father's family. I was given some information that was fascinating to me, and I wanted to know more about his life. I never knew my father's father, or his mother. I have a picture of his mother and now know why my mother always called me Lizzy Gross, my father's mother. I look just like her. Coming from such a large family, there is so much to learn on both my father and my mother's side. These two individuals were strong people, and during the time they were living and raising so many children, I can imagine that things were rough for them, but they prevailed.

I read somewhere that we blot things out of our minds that make us feel bad or guilty, as if they never happened. I believe as human beings we take so much for granted. As I am writing this, I am finally realizing the great sacrifice that my mother made for me by taking my children, all four of them when they were born, and taking care of them. What a wonderful person this lady was, and I have much love and respect for her.

Down through the years, there were times when I would lie in bed late at night and I pray to God to forgive me for some of the things that I had done, that I knew were the wrong things to do. I asked Him to forgive me for cheating my children out of having a decent father figure in their lives. I would lie quietly and wait for an answer from God. When I felt peace come over me, I would slip into a deep sleep. Mr. Joseph Scriven wrote this song when I imagine he was feeling the same as me: "O what peace we often forfeit, O what needless pain we bear, all because we do not carry; everything to God in prayer."

One day I was listening to a preacher on the radio, something that I do regularly. Pastor David Jeremiah, Pastor Tony Evans, and Pastor Michael Youssef come on the radio every morning on 105.1. I can't remember which one said, "How dare you continue to ask God for forgiveness over and over again. He heard you the first time. The Bible tells us if we confess our sins, He is faithful and just to forgive us our sins, and cleanse us from all unrighteousness." I do believe that we serve a God who keeps His word and cannot lie. If we really believe that, why do we keep asking Him for the same things over and over again?

As I get older, I find myself thinking of my mortality. I know that my time here on earth is limited, and I need to get myself in the frame of mind to think of how I live my life. I try to treat others as I want to be treated. I tell my family that I love them every chance I get. I show my love to others as much as I can. Our Bible tells us in Romans 12:2, "Don't copy the behavior and customs of this world, but let God transform us into a new person by changing the way we think. Then we will know what God wants us to do, and we will know how good and pleasing and perfect His will really is."

I find that it is not easy to live a godly life. There are so many obstacles that stand in our way. Anyone who says it is easy hasn't lived as long as I have, or they just don't care how they live. I want to live a life that God will be pleased with so that my name can be written in the Book of Life. I want to go to heaven to live with my Lord, and I am striving toward that mark. I realize that the road that I am on is not as straight as I would like it to be. I also know that God has not brought me this far to leave me.

My daughter questioned me one day as to why I have not moved. I moved into my home in December of 1969 and I am still living here. I had the opportunity to move a few times. Both times when I had to move out because of fire, I decided to have my home repaired and move back in. One of the main reasons I never wanted to move is because I would have lost contact with a lot of folks I wanted to see again. All of those folks know my address. I am afraid that if they decided to stop by to see if I am still living there and I am not, we would miss seeing each other.

It is just so strange that a lot of people that I was very close to, I have lost contact with. Some have moved away and I haven't seen them in years.

I don't know if a lot of them are still living or not. I certainly hope they are, and one day they will stop by and say, "Hi, Mary, I was hoping that you still lived here." My daughter tells people that I will never move, and maybe she is right—I have no desire to move.

I raised all four of my children in this house, and now that they are all grown up and have homes of their own, I am both satisfied and very grateful to God for giving me this house. He has blessed me to be able to live here and raise my children in our two-bedroom, full-basement modest home. I don't know what the future holds for me, but I am at peace here and pray that God will continue to be merciful unto me until He decides what will happen to me in the future. Every week I get a phone call or a letter telling me they want to buy my home. I have no intention of moving or selling my home.

I am writing this at the age of seventy. A lot of folks would probably feel that it's too late to embark upon a new career, or any tangible thing that will be lasting. However, I am praying to the Holy Spirit. I am asking Him to lead and guide me toward something that I can do for the further building of His Kingdom. I am waiting for an answer. My Bible tells me to wait on the Lord and be of good courage; and He will direct my path. I believe that with all my heart, and I will be obedient to His will and way! I have come a long way by God directing my path, and I don't believe that He has brought me this far to leave me now.

As I look back over my life at the age of seventy years, I am trying to think of those whom I can honestly say influenced and encouraged me. My mother was the greatest example for me to be the responsible person that I am today.

She didn't go too far in school, but she was one of the smartest people I have ever known. She had common sense. I find myself doing and saying some of the same things to my children that she said to us as we were growing up. I always wondered how she knew where everything was in the house. If you asked her where the needle and thread were, she was able to tell you. One day I asked her how she knew where everything was. She said, "If you put them back where you got them from, you will know where to find them." Something as simple as that really impressed me. I never really thought of it that way!

When I was in elementary school, Mrs. Bullard, our music teacher, was very encouraging to me. She would always call on me to lead or learn a new song. She would choose me to sing a solo at different functions at the school. She told me that I had a great voice, and I should practice as much as I could to strengthen it and one day it would carry me very far. I believed her and I sang whenever and wherever I could.

The Bible tells us that man should always pray without ceasing, because prayer changes things. I find myself praying more now than ever.

I pray for my children, my grandchildren, my great-grandbabies, and myself. I pray for my siblings and their families. I pray for my church family, my community, and the world we live in. The older I get, the more I realize just how important and necessary it is for us to pray and get closer to God, who is the author and finisher of our faith. I am seeing things that are going on around me that I have never seen before. I shudder to think that it will get worse, but I know within my heart and soul that things surely will.

I began to read the books of Daniel and Revelation. It gets a bit scary to read what will happen, but I also know that reading those books will help keep me trying to live the best life that I can on this earth. God commands that we love one another. I have not seen in the Bible that He tells us to like one another. Let's face it, some folks make it very hard to like them, but we have to love them because God is love. I have always thought that we should give people the benefit of doubt. Dr. Phil says that we shouldn't, because the world has changed and people do not deserve to be given the benefit of doubt. That is where we differ.

I know that there are things about me that I can change, and it's not always the other person's fault. I have standoff ways about myself until I get to know someone better. I don't believe in jumping in and trying to make friends when meeting someone. I believe some take that as being snobbish, but I am just being careful. Too bad I didn't do that with a few of my suitors. There were a few times when I felt that I could jump in and share my thoughts and feelings with others. I know now that it was the Holy Spirit that led me to feel that way. To this day, those folks are still my friends. There is not a day that goes by that I don't ask the Holy Spirit to lead, guide, and direct me through the day. I ask God to order my steps and the steps of my family and friends.

As far back as I can remember, I have always enjoyed the pleasure of being alone. There are some who need to always be around or with someone. I am just the opposite. Except for raising and being around my children, I have spent a lot of time alone, and to this day that is true. I have read many books and saw many stories of folks who would literally do anything to be around others most of their time. I really do not feel that way. I am comfortable and content to be alone with myself.

Now that my children are all grown up and have homes of their own, I am content to be living alone to do and be who I am as a person, and as a mother of grandchildren and great-grandchildren. I love them to visit with me, and when they leave to return to their homes, I always pray to the good Lord that He will give them traveling grace and mercy while on dangerous highways. Then I relax to a peaceful, quiet existence.

Coming from a large family helps me to appreciate quiet times. I love to read and think. Being alone gives me the opportunity to do both of those things. I also enjoy being alone while driving. I love to pick out my most enjoyable CDs, and as long as I have good music, I can drive for miles and never get tired. Although I have heard the songs over and over again, I still don't like the distractions and interruptions I get when someone else is riding with me and talking and asking me questions when there is a certain part of the music that I want to hear. A lot of times I won't even answer, hoping they will get the message and stop talking. Traveling home to see my sisters and brothers is a great joy for me. I moved away from home a very long time ago, but I make it my business to go home often to see my siblings and their families.

I know some folks that wouldn't dream of going to a movie, a show, or out to dinner alone, but I am not one of those. If I feel like going out, I go and enjoy being out doing what I like to do. I just enjoy being with me.

I am a dreamer, so I dream alone a lot! That is not to say that I never go out with others, because I do, but it must be with people I really enjoy being around. I don't drink a lot and I don't smoke, so that is a factor of not being around folks who do.

I had been so active in my younger years that the *Young and the Restless* has nothing on me. This makes me appreciate the quiet times at the age that I am now.

I don't feel that I am missing out on too much, but there are things I want to do before my life is over.

I get joy when I am doing something for someone else. I am a servant, and I want to live a servant's life. My old friend John finally retired after forty-five years of government service and I attended his ceremony. I had the pleasure of speaking on the time of reflections, and I wanted him to know that there is life after retirement.

One day a friend told me that I was outspoken. He said that he admired that. I never thought of myself as being opinionated, but I am known for speaking out on what I think is the truth. I believe in calling things as I see them. Perhaps that doesn't go over well with some, but I don't mean it to be mean; I only speak on what I see and feel. Be it in my job, in the church, or in my home, I tell it like it is, but there are family members who take offense to some of the things I say and do.

I started receiving calls from an institution that one of my grandsons was incarcerated in. The voice on the answering service said that I had to become eligible to receive these calls by giving them my credit card number. I declined to do so and hung up the phone. I received about three of these calls before I called his mother. I told her the next time she talked with him, tell him that if he wanted to speak with me, stay out of jail, and come by my house and we can talk as long as he wanted to.

I am sure that didn't go over well with her. However, I saw my grandson walking down the street one day and found out that he had been released from jail. I waved to him. He looked puzzled to see me, and I expect that he wasn't too excited because he knew that I saw him, and he also knew that he didn't try to contact me or come to see me upon his release.

My son told me that he tried to bring him over to see me and he refused. It wasn't long after that that I heard that he was locked up again. He wants me to accept collect calls from prison and pay to talk with him. I love my grandchildren very much, but I will not be a part of enabling them to continue to do wrong and be rewarded for it.

Another instance is one of my daughters-in-law not speaking to me because she didn't like something I said to my son regarding some difficulties they were having. She read something I wrote to him through e-mail and she took offense to it. She only read part of what I said to him, but the part that she read she didn't like. She has known me a very long time, and she knew that whatever happened, although I don't hold my children up in wrongdoing, I still will not desert or put them down either. He asked my advice on the matter and I gave it. What he had done was wrong. However, I felt that we all make mistakes. Even she has made a few, and neither he nor I held it against her. I am hoping that one day soon we will be able to talk about it and put it to rest. If we cannot do that, we will go on with our lives. I raised three sons and one daughter. I realize that boys greatly need a man to raise them to become men.

My sons didn't have the steady guidance of a man in our home. I had to be both mother and father, which is impossible to do. So my sons had a hard time adjusting to rules of what a young boy was supposed to do and be, and the proper way they should be brought up to be a man. I did the best that I could under the circumstances, but I made mistakes. Although my sons didn't have a male figure to raise them, they had eight uncles they emulated.

However, they also had fathers who weren't perfect, and I realize they also had some of the characteristics of their fathers.

I was the major person in their lives when I was a young woman raising sons. They loved and respected me, as they could see that I was doing the best I could to raise them. They knew I loved them more than anything in this world, and I still do. Because they love and respect me, they show the women they married the same respect they showed me. They were taught to love their wives as the Bible taught.

I also understand that some women in this world haven't grown up with fathers in their home, either. So they see how their mama treated men. Some were not used to men treating them with respect and caring for them, as a man should. My sons respect me and love me. They know how to treat a woman and attempted to show their wives how much they loved them. Some women didn't understand that. When a man was kind, thoughtful, and gentle to them, they confused that as being weak and timid. So they felt they should take the lead in the relationship. When they grew up, they did the only thing they knew how to do and that was to treat men the way they saw their mother treat men. Some women are emasculators of men and really don't know how to treat them. I witnessed that with my sons. My feeling was: I have already raised these men; they don't need to be raised again by their wives. And I let them know that.

I know that I am not perfect, not by a long shot. As you read my story, you can see that, but I believe in transparency, even if it is me I am talking about. I will always respect another human being. That's who I am as a person, but I don't like phony-acting people. I believe we should all be who we are and not try to impress others to make ourselves look good in someone else's eyes.

I have a dog named Corky. He wasn't with me long before he knew what I meant when I spoke to him. He understands every word I say and he obeys me accordingly. He understands that I am the one he depends on to feed and care for him, so he treats me with respect—and he is a dog.

God made all of us and I believe He did a great job. I am amazed at people who get all kinds of things done to their bodies because they don't like the way they look. I feel that this is a slap in God's face to tell Him,

"I don't like the way You made me." There are things we do to enhance our looks such as makeup, but facelifts and total body changes I believe are an abomination to our Lord. These are my beliefs and my feelings. I am not trying to tell anyone else how to feel.

When I look in the mirror, I speak to my mother because I look just like her. I have no problem with that at all. I only pray that I have a heart like hers, because she was one of the gentlest and kindest persons I have ever known. God truly blessed us with a wonderful strong and humble mother, and I thank Him for that every day.

While writing this book at the age of seventy, I did a lot of reflecting over my life. I cannot help but give God praises for the life that He has allowed me to live on this earth, knowing that He is not finished with me yet. God promised me that He would never leave, nor forsake me, and I believe that His word is true. When I think about some of the accomplishments I have achieved during the years, I thank God because I know that it wasn't anybody but Him who had brought me thus far. I obtained, overcame, and completed things that I would never have if God were not on my side, leading and guiding me.

I recall the time that I bought this ice cream truck and decided I was going into business for myself. When I bought the truck, I didn't really think things through the way I should have.

It didn't work out too well, but I felt proud that I was able to get through all the government red tape. I fixed that truck up. Afterward, I was approved by the District government and received my papers to go into business on the street to sell my product. A friend of mine by the name of Mac came over and put running water in it for me. I went over to Bladensburg Road where the merchandise was sold to those of us who had trucks on the street, and filled it with ice cream, candy, gum, and all the stuff folks buy from trucks. I even had a fence built in my backyard with a gate so I could park the truck at night and plug it into my house to keep the ice cream frozen.

The first day I drove the truck I went up town on 14th Street, NW, where the construction workers were. Mac had cooked some ribs for me to sell, but no one bought any. I was new to everyone and I didn't get much business that day. I sold a few sodas and some ice cream. Since I had a full-time job, I knew that I had to find someone to drive my truck as I was working every day.

Mac told me that he had spoken to his cousin David, and he agreed to drive for me. I had to pick him up in the morning before I went to work and bring him over to my house to pick up the truck. He would then drive the truck back to where he lived. David wanted to be paid on a daily basis. I later learned that he would keep the truck parked in front of his house all day, and later when the kids would get out of school, he would open the truck for business.

After paying him off daily and not even breaking even as far as money goes, I decided that it wasn't working out and I let him go. Later I put a "For Sale" sign on the truck and got a response. The man who bought the truck had a big smile on his face when he drove away.

Although things didn't work out well as far as being an entrepreneur, I felt that I had accomplished something. At least I made it work for a while. It was not easy working through the bureaucracy of the District government, but I did it.

I called my cousin Sherwood and told him what happened. He said he would have taken the truck and worked it for me if he knew about it. I am sure he would have, but it just wasn't in the cards, I suppose. Later when I reflected on it, I realized that the mistake I made was "putting the cart before the horse," as the older folks would say. I really didn't think it through. My plan was to get my sons involved, so I named our company

"B & W Express," which stood for Brown and Washington. But my sons had other plans, and they did not include driving an ice cream truck.

Once I make up my mind to do something, nothing can stop me. The problem that I have is making up my mind. The hardest thing for me is to stay focused. I have so many ideas of things I would like to do, but I know that I have to have patience and stay focused on one thing at a time. At the ripe age of seventy, I thank God that I am in relatively good health. I have a few aches and pains here and there, and a little arthritis in my knees. But I won't let that stop me from achieving my goals.

I feel blessed that I am not the worst looking person in the world. I can still smile and feel good about myself. I pray to God every day to thank Him for allowing me to see another day. I also ask Him to teach me to number my days, so that I can do His will, and to give me the tolerance that I need to have for others.

I just can't stand folks murmuring all the time about everything and just plain acting stupid. For some, nothing is ever going right in their lives. Some are just ignorant. However, I know that ignorance is not something that folks want to have—sometimes they just don't know any better. I want to be, and I know that I have to be, more understanding and forgiving of those folks. I know if I am obedient to His will and His way, one day He will tell me, "Well done, my good and faithful servant, you have been faithful over a few things. I will make you ruler over many."

I will always do my best to be kind and thoughtful to others. I will do all that I can to help my fellow man, and I will always love and honor the Lord our Savior, Jesus the Christ. Every opportunity I get, I talk with my children and grandbabies about going to church and asking the Lord Jesus into their lives. I feel strongly that it is my duty as a Christian to do all that I can to lead my family to Christ Jesus.

I don't find that a hard thing to do because our dear mother was that kind of a lady and she taught us well, both daughters and sons. I see how my brothers treat their wives with so much love and respect. I noticed how my oldest sister hung in there with her late husband for many years, and my sister Tina and her husband just celebrated their 50th wedding anniversary last year. I have not been so lucky with the male gender, but I will not complain. I am still hopeful that God will send someone into my life that I deserve and someone who deserves me.

I am so thankful and most grateful to our Savior for the many blessings that have been bestowed upon my family and me. Floyd has made me so proud of him. Once he got involved in the church, he never looked back. He is now Elder Floyd A. Washington and preaches at his church sometimes. He is a wonderful speaker.

Juan had a rough life as a young man. He was robbed many times, shot in his right leg, and strung out on drugs. But I prayed to the Lord and He heard my cry. Juan endured through many trials and tribulations as a young man.

Even though he found himself in many dangerous situations, God brought him through them all. God knew Juan's heart. He has a heart of Christ. He is one of the kindest human beings I have ever had the pleasure to know. Even though there are haters who have crossed his path, God found favor in him and continues to bless my son. God is a God of second chances and He restored my son. Now he has the keys to both of the Galilee Baptist churches and goes to work there every day. He also works part time for Safeway. He has a very nice apartment, and he bought all the furniture he needed before moving in. He will never take anything from anyone. He is very happy with his girlfriend Karen. His daughter Brittany stays with them on some weekends.

Gregg returned from serving in the military (army) after twenty years, bought a home located in Columbia, South Carolina, and went to college and earned a degree. He has his own lawn company and is fully employed with the Department of Veteran Affairs.

Lori is married and a mother and grandmother. She owns her home, has a job as a contractor for the Department of Justice, and is doing well.

Why on earth would I complain? I heard this song one day when I was feeling a little down. It was a song by a lady named Denice Williams. She is called the "song bird" because her voice sounds like a bird singing. The song she was singing was "Black Butterfly." It touched me to my very core and I cried and cried. The next day I got a tattoo of a black butterfly just above my left breast, representing my four children.

I think part of my thoughts were about how far we had come as a family, and me as a single mother raising three sons and a daughter. The other emotions were just knowing that I was never alone—God was always there with us, carrying us through it all, so most of the tears were tears of joy and gratefulness to Him!

So far, I have had a good life. That is, the good has outweighed the bad. I've had my share of ups and downs, but my ups far outweigh my downs. I attribute that to being me, just being real about who I am. I have always liked myself, not to the point of arrogance, but just always felt that I was okay with who I was. There are those who don't care too much for me, but I never let those individuals bother me. I believe it's not my problem. The problem belongs to them.

When I told some of my friends and family I was writing a book, they were very encouraging. They thought it was such a great idea. Some folks even asked me to make sure I let them know when it was published so they could get a copy. That made me feel good, as I really didn't expect that type of response. It let me know they thought my life was interesting enough to read about. That gave me the incentive to really get into the spirit of writing.

I want to talk about my great-grandson Darrell. He is my granddaughter Tamia's son and my daughter Lori's grandson. He makes me look at life in such a special way. As I am writing this, he is nine years old. He will be ten years old on October 28. I have two great-grandsons who were born on October 28. The other one is Jamari Tyrell, and he is the grandson of my son Juan and the son of Juan Jr., my grandson.

As I spend time around those two boys, I thank the Lord every day for His supernatural power. Those young boys are so intelligent it's scary. When I am talking to Darrell, I am amazed how intelligent he is.

At times, I prefer being with him and talking with him more than being with grown folks. Both of those young boys have so much wisdom to be so young, such common sense. They both are quick to learn and knowledgeable on so many subjects.

The Bible speaks of a wiser generation, and I truly believe this is the generation that the Bible speaks of. I long to be around all of my grand- and great-grandchildren. However, I have to wait until the mothers of the children decide that it is important enough to bring them around. I love them all, but I decided not to interfere with how they are raising their families, and I pray that one day they will realize I could be a very significant part in their lives.

I spend more time with Darrell because his mother, Tamia, brings him around me often. I have been watching and listening to him since he was born. I noticed at a very young age just how intelligent he was. There is not a subject that you speak on that he doesn't know something about, be it sports, movies, computers, or technology. He can hold an intelligent conversation on all those things.

He called me one day and said, "GG, my mother told me that you were writing a book."

I said, "Yes, I am Darrell."

He asked, "Am I going to be in your book?"

I told him yes.

He said, "When you get through writing it, I want to read it."

I promised that I would give him a copy, and I intend to do just that. He is in the third grade and can read better than a lot of folks I know. I thank God for allowing me to live to see and spend time with my babies.

I don't know if my life is that interesting or not, but I do know that what I am writing is real and true. I also believe that some will be able to relate to what my life has been about and know that they are not the only ones who experienced the same things that I have experienced in my life—the good, the bad, and the ugly.

God has been good to my entire family. Our family started out with me the ninth of thirteen children—four sisters and eight brothers. There are ten of us left on this earth, and we are eternally grateful. We love each other dearly. I thank God for such a large and loving family that He has blessed me with.

My plan for the near future is to earn a college degree, get involved in our government, and try to make our city a better place to live by getting the homeless children and their parents out of shelters and into affordable housing. My prayer is that God will continue to watch over me and give me the strength and the wisdom I need to stay focused and do His will.

I have learned so much in my years of living on this earth. I mostly realize that we shouldn't take ourselves so seriously, and learn to laugh at ourselves more. Things are not that bad if we seek to find the positive things in life. I believe we should wake up every morning with a smile on our faces, realizing first of all that we woke up and what a blessing that is. So many others didn't wake up. I love to go to sleep at night because I look forward to the dreams I will have. I have wonderful dreams and can't wait to find out what my next dream will be about.

We should thank God for the angels He sent to watch over us while we are sleeping, and who touch us with a finger of love to wake us up to see another day. God promised us new mercies every morning, and for that alone, we should be grateful.

Then we should ask, "God, what will You have me to do this day to be a blessing to someone else?" If we ask Him this question with honesty and conviction, I promise you He will answer. You will find yourself going through the day feeling strong, happy, and peaceful.

The Bible tells us to "Trust in the Lord with all of our heart, and lean not to our own understanding, but in all of our ways, acknowledge Him and He will direct our path." God's word is true, and He really means what He says. We cannot continually read and repeat that verse, like a lot of us do, and not trust and put our faith in God's word. We have to trust in God and find out if He really means what He is saying to us.

I have lived long enough to know that He is the only one we can put our trust in, so why not take Him at His word and try Him? I'll be the first one to say that I haven't always felt this way. But I know that I have tried everything else and it didn't necessarily work. So I say, why not try God? It surely can't hurt. I can honestly tell you, if you put your trust in Him, things may not always work the way you think they will, but the way God works things out will blow your mind.

Trying to tell some people about Christ Jesus is like putting a cross in front of Satan's face—they just don't want to hear or receive what you are saying—but we have to keep trying without banging them over the head with a Bible. Jesus said, "If I be lifted up on this earth, I'll draw all men unto me." We just have a charge to lift Jesus up and He will surely do the rest.

I think that we, as Christians who profess to love God, have to set an example by the way we live the life we talk and sing about. When I think of the goodness of Jesus and all that He has done for me, I can't help but praise Him.

He has brought my family and me through so much, and we will be eternally grateful to Him and will continue to sing His praise. Whenever I have the opportunity to join together with my family, we sing praises to God because we know what He has brought us through. I remember the words of the hymn that was written by John Newton, a slave owner:

> Amazing grace, how sweet the sound
> That saved a wretch like me!
> I once was lost, but now am found,
> Was blind but now I see!
>
> 'Twas grace that taught my heart to fear,
> And grace my fears relieved;
> How precious did that grace appear?
> The hour I first believed!
>
> Thru many dangers, toils and snares
> I have already come,
> 'tis grace hath brought me safe thus far,
> And grace will lead me home.
>
> When we've been there ten thousand years,
> Bright shining as the sun,
> We've no less days to sing God's praise
> Than when we'd first begun.

What would we do if we didn't have God on our side? I often think of that, but I shudder to think of what or where we would be. I have learned a lot in my life, and I know beyond a shadow of a doubt that we need to pray more. We are living in a sinful world. When Adam disobeyed God, he opened up this earth for Satan to roam, devour, and destroy, and that is what he's doing on this earth today. I know that if we join forces and pray more, we can conquer Satan's vices, and God will have mercy on us and make Satan leave us alone. I will continue to pray for that until I die. While I am still living in this world, I know that it is my responsibility to lift up the name of Jesus so that He may draw all men unto Him.

At the beginning of this story, I spoke about hope. Now I want to speak on prayer and how it should manifest itself in our very existence. God operates in our lives through prayer. Prayer unlocks the key to our victory in Christ Jesus.

Satan is so devious. He has ways of keeping us so busy, thinking we are working for God, that we don't take the time to pray. We say a prayer at bedtime before we go to sleep, or maybe when we wake up in the morning, or when trouble comes our way.

Other times, we are busy trying to figure out how we can make more money to buy more stuff, so we lose out on the opportunity to pray because we have so many other things distracting us. That is the trick of the devil.

We buy bestselling religious books and tapes, and we listen to preachers on the radio. All that is fine in its place, but we lose out on the opportunity of taking the time to pray. But the Bible tells us that man should always pray without ceasing, for prayer changes things.

"Oh taste and see that the Lord is good" (Psalm 34:8).

"How sweet are your words to my taste, sweeter than honey to my mouth" (Psalm 119:103).

Many of us really don't use the power that God put in our hands, and that power is prayer. We have to pray to God, pray for self and family, and pray against the tricks of Satan. Yes, prayer is our weapon. I feel sad when our prayer ministry has prayer vigils at the church and there is not a large turnout. We only have it four times a year, for one hour. You would think that the church would be full, but I don't remember seeing more than twenty people there each time. I feel that the church should be full like the 11:00 a.m. Sunday service is. In perilous times such as these, we need to be collectively praying every chance we get and as often as we can.

We only get to live this life once, and I believe we are obligated to live it to the best of our ability.

I am sure there will be those who say I wasn't an angel, and I will be the first to agree, but we all have a past and no one on this earth is perfect. I heard someone say, "We are all X something." The most we can do is live our lives the best we can by treating others the way we would want to be treated.

A long time ago, I did something that changed my life forever, and I know now that was the best thing I could have done. It was to answer the call and walk down to the altar and accept Christ Jesus as my Lord and Savior. I did that at our church in 1982, and I haven't regretted doing it.

The Bible tells us to "Be diligent to present ourselves approved to God, a worker who does not need to be ashamed, rightly dividing the word of truth" (2 Timothy 2:15).

If we are obedient to God's will and way, He will direct our paths and show us how to live the best life we can while we are on this side of the world. I can sing with honesty and conviction, "I am redeemed, bought with a price; Jesus has changed my whole life."

I thank God every day and will for the rest of my life. There will always be those who will say I knew her/him when… But if we make the decision to put God first in our lives and live the way that He commands of us to live, we can all change and live a better life and become new creatures in Christ.

"For by grace you have been saved through faith, and that not of yourselves; it is the gift of God, not of works, lest anyone should boast" (Ephesians 2:8).

My life is an open book and I am not ashamed of it or the things that happened in it. I believed that what happened to me was supposed to happen. Are there some things that I would change if I could? Of course there are, but I cannot change them, so I accept the fact that I have no control over my life, but God has, and I am satisfied in knowing that. If I start to regret things that happened in the past, I would regret having my children whom I love dearly, and I wouldn't have the pleasure of my grandchildren who are the loves of my life.

I am too blessed to start feeling sorry for myself. Things could be a lot worse than they are, but God has always watched over me. He allowed some things to happen to me for reasons that only He knows. I don't believe that we will ever understand all the things that God allows to happen to us. Maybe we will never know until He is ready to reveal it. We all have flaws, but we are all made in His image and that is a good thing. God wants us to put our trust and faith in Him. He will work things out for our good because He promised that no good thing would He withheld from us.

"We all are being transformed by the spirit of the Lord" (2 Corinthians 3:18).

I'll never forget the day I turned forty years old. I was extremely depressed. That evening, I was literally crying out loud. I was home alone. I really didn't understand what was happening to me. To this very day, I still cannot tell you what was going on.

A knock came at the door. I opened it and there stood my brother Lincoln. He had a bottle of wine with him. I hugged him and laughed and hugged him again. He spent the entire evening with me, and we just talked and enjoyed each other.

He made me so happy just to see him standing there. I don't think I told him how I was feeling before he came, but I know it changed me in a positive way. I love my sisters and brothers so much!

My life is a lot easier, and I am more at peace now within because I know that God loves me, and as I embrace God's word more and more, I want to honor Him more and more. The day I turned fifty I was so happy I just felt like I had finally arrived! Go figure!

"Be steadfast, immovable, always abounding in the work of the Lord, knowing that my labor is not in vain in the Lord" (Corinthians 15:58).

I don't know if there is someone for me to live my life with as a companion, but I hear that there is someone for everyone in this world. I am going to be led by the Spirit and see where it takes me or whom it brings me. I haven't given up hope of having a real relationship or companion in my life, but this time I will wait on the Lord to choose him for me and not the other way around.

Our Bible tells us that a man who finds a good wife finds a good thing. I will wait until he finds me, and even if he doesn't, I will be okay. Everyone who is alone is not necessarily lonely. I am at peace with my life and myself. I am always in awe of the greatness of God and how He moves in my life. When we hear folks say that God works in mysterious ways, believe it—it's true.

Earlier I spoke of being sad each time I found out I was pregnant, but as I look back over my life, I know that God had a purpose for me. Years later, I felt strongly about feeding young families. I thought of myself and how it was to try my best to take care of my children. Some days I wondered how I was going to feed them that day. The good Lord always made a way for me. As I would drive up and down the streets of Washington, DC, and see young mothers with their babies. I would think, *That was once me. Does she need help feeding those babies the same as I did?* Every day I would pray to the Holy Spirit and ask Him to please put someone in my path that I could bless that day. I would continue to see these young women with their babies. That's when I knew what I had to do. My ministry would be feeding the needy, and I have been doing that now for thirteen years. I knew that this was the Holy Spirit leading me!

One evening, our pastor Dr. Lloyd T. McGriff preached on the one hundred Psalms and his title was "Do Your Part!" I believe that we all have an obligation to do our part in this life. Some of us just don't know what our part is. We have to call on the Holy Spirit and ask what our part is. The Holy Spirit promised to lead and guide us to all truth. All we have to do is ask, seek, and knock.

I stopped complaining about things that happen and things that have happened in my life as I go from day to day. We have to live the best life we can, always reading and studying the word of God, so that we can understand what God expects of us.

We all have a part to play; we just have to find out what our part is. Try doing a good deed for someone every chance you get. Some may think it has to be something big, but it doesn't have to be. Someone may be feeling down and just need a smile, a hug, or time to listen to them. Someone may ask you to pray for them or someone in their family. Whenever that happens, stop whatever you are doing and pray for them. My mission is to minister to my family and lead them to Christ. We are big on our family getting together not only for big family reunions but for any reason.

I make it a priority to take advantage of those times and minister to them and talk about Jesus Christ. I want my children and my children's children to seek first the kingdom of God and His righteousness. I want to go to heaven and see all my family members there also.

Our Bible tells us that the earth is the Lord's and the fullness thereof. In other words, He created everything and us. Pastor Billy Graham said, "That though we may not be able to see his purpose or his plan, the Lord of heaven is on his throne and in firm control of the universe and our lives, so we entrust him with our future."

In the book of Acts 17:26, it tells us that "God has made from one blood every nation of men to dwell on all the face of the earth." That means that we are all equal, and neither race nor ethnicity is superior or inferior to another.

I believe in my heart that all the answers to every question we have can be found in the Bible. God's word is indeed a lamp unto our feet and a light unto our path. We just have to be obedient to God's will and way. In 1 Samuel 15:22, it tells us that to obey is better than sacrifice.

A man by the name of Randy Kilgore wrote on the Christian blog *Our Daily Bread*, "When the trials of today seem more daunting than your strength, let the Lord show you the end of the story when you will be in His presence forever!"

The more time we spend in God's word and in prayer, we can keep our connection alive with him, then we will be willing to be doers of his word and not just sayers (James 1:22–24).

I also believe that some of the ways we can make God smile are to:

(A) Learn how to laugh at ourselves and stop taking ourselves so seriously.

(B) Do good things while no one else is looking. God sees.

(C) If you make a promise to someone or a commitment, do all you can to keep it.

(D) Remember that it's not always about you. Don't always expect to be the front and center of everything.

(E) If you wake up in the morning after a night's sleep, you are doing a lot better than millions of others. Be grateful and thank God.

(F) Smile, things could be a lot worse!

(G) A good godly person doesn't put others down in order to lift themselves up. God gave us all gifts and talents. What God has for you is for you!

One of the ways I stay grounded is looking at the family pictures I have on my walls. There are pictures everywhere in my home. They are in the dining room, the living room, the basement, and my bedrooms. I often walk around touching the pictures and praying for the individual in that particular frame.

I start by thanking God for that individual. I feel so blessed knowing that most of those who are in the pictures started with me. I am mother, grandmother, and great-grandmother to most of them. Then I look at my extended family and friends. I just marvel at what a mighty God we serve! Those are the things that keep me seeking to do better and aspire to live a better life.

We were engaged in a conversation at our Vacation Bible School class regarding single women. One of the ladies asked for prayers for her sister who decided to commit suicide because she felt that her relationship with her boyfriend was at an end and she didn't want to be alone. Hearing that broke my heart, as I could relate to part of what was said. I never felt that I wanted to kill myself, but there were times when I felt I couldn't go on without my man. It was years ago when I felt that way. I have lived without a man in my life for several years now, and I am doing just fine. I may be alone, but I am not lonely. There is a difference. I am at peace with God and myself. When I think of the many times that I was with a man, some of those times were not so peaceful.

If I were asked to speak to women on this subject, I would tell them to not make men their all and all. Only Christ should be their all and all.

Ever since I gave my heart to Jesus and put Him first in my life, I have been a happy, contented, and peaceful woman. I am grateful to be alive and in good health in my seventies. I will not waste the precious time that I have left on this earth feeling sorry for myself or feeling depressed, especially about things that are beyond my control. God has been too good to me to be ungrateful, and He has shown my entire family and me His favor.

Our God is sovereign. His ways are not our ways, nor His thoughts our thoughts. There is no other like Him and there will never be. He is everywhere. He knows everything. He counts every hair on our heads and every tear that falls from our eyes.

Mr. Bill Crowder wrote these words on *Our Daily Bread*: "There is no safe, risk-free environment in which we can experience life's ups and downs unharmed. The risks and dangers of living in a broken world are inescapable. That's why the words of Jesus are so reassuring."

Jesus said, "These things I have spoken to you, that in me you may have peace. In the world you will have tribulation; but be of good cheer, I have overcome the world" (John 16:33).

This is the good news of our Lord and Savior! Although we can't avoid the dangers of life in a fallen world, we can have peace through a relationship with Jesus. "He has secured our ultimate victory. No life is more secured than a life surrendered to God" I read that sentence in the book of Our Daily Bread.

I would be remiss if I didn't speak about a beautiful young lady by the name of Euphoria Mason-Wills. For a long time, I had heard that she was telling folks, "When I grow up, I want to be like Mary Washington." When I heard this for the first time, I sort of laughed it off. But then I heard it again. She is a now a full-grown woman and is still telling people that.

Now, I would be lying if I said that I wasn't flattered at the thought she felt that way about me, but I often wondered why she wanted to be like me. What had I done to make her feel that way? I knew that it had to be something positive in order for her to even think that way.

On April 8, 1958, our school, Brooks High, was invited to appear on the *Milt Grant Show*. It was a television show that invited high school students to come on and dance. I was invited to go with this guy named McDaniel Rawlings. When it was time for the dance contest, I danced with a guy named Carl Griffin. We won the contest and were given a certificate for a pair of Tom McCann shoes. I will never forget that long ride home on the bus that evening. There were couples who felt they could dance a lot better than we could, and that was true, but they didn't win. The older students were angry, but the younger students were proud and happy for us. I believe that Euphoria was one of the proud and happy ones.

I saw her at a funeral not too long ago, and she came up to me and hugged me. She told me that she still felt that way—she wanted to be just like me. I said to her, "Thank you for feeling that way. I am flattered, but don't try to be like me, try to be like Jesus. That's who I'm trying to be like." We hugged and said good-bye. On my way home, I thought what a nice lady she was. I had to have shown her something that was positive and I thanked God for that. I realize that it's not so much what you say, it's how you live and what others see in you that make them want to be like you.

Every year we try to get together and honor someone in our family to let them know how much we love and appreciate them. One year my family honored me and my sister Tina.

We also celebrated both of our deceased brothers before they passed away, Buddy and Clarence. One year we honored our sister Ree. We honored them because we wanted to show our appreciation for the lives they lived, showing love and kindness to us all. This year we are honoring our brother Milford.

I strongly believe that we should give flowers to those who can still see, smell, and appreciate them, and not wait until they are lying in a casket and can't hear or appreciate the nice things we do or say about them. After all, they are dead.

When I think of Milford, I just can't help but smile. He never ceases to amaze me. He's a hardworking man, and always has been. When he was younger, he had an opportunity to play professional baseball. Unfortunately, he was involved in an accident and hurt his arm. Most of my brothers were fine baseball players. I don't remember Milford going to church much in the earlier years. When he did start to go, he never stopped. He loves the Lord and promised to serve Him for the rest of his life. He also took up where my mother left off by bringing candy mints to church and sharing them with anyone who wanted one.

Candy is not the only thing that Milford gives away. Every time we gather for our reunions, Milford asks us to line up and he hands each one of us a hundred-dollar bill. A few times there were twelve of us who lined up, and we all received a hundred-dollar bill. He enjoys giving to others and showing his love for us every chance he gets. He has the heart of our mother and deserves to be honored.

I am now about to come to the end of my story. I continue to pray that God will bless that day of celebration, and this will be the beginning of a new era in the lives of the younger members of our family so they will continue to keep the honors and the celebrations going for years to come.

Summary

As a young naïve woman, I made many mistakes. Some of my actions were indeed intentional, some weren't. Some I understood, some I had no understanding of. But there is one thing I know and that is this:

I didn't create myself. God created me, and I don't believe that He has ever made a mistake. I believe that everything that happened to me was ordained before I was even conceived in my mother's womb. I am who I am and what I am today because of what happened in the past. Now I realize that I had to be under the authority of God in order for Him to dispatch angels to watch over me. But I, like many others, were ignorant and didn't have knowledge or understanding of His word. So I leaned unto my own understanding. But I thank God today for His word, and I have gained knowledge and understanding. We all have a past and my story is not too different from some others. Some of our stories are good, and some are not so good.

However, we all have had to endure something that has made us what we are today and had no control over. The plan that God had for me materialized in my life and in the lives of my children for reasons that only He knows.

This I believe. I won't hold grudges in my heart for anyone, not even for those who abused me in the past. One thing I know for sure is that people can change, and I am a prime example of that fact.

Everything that happens to us happens for a reason. The answer for everything we experienced on this earth, we can find in the Bible, in the word of God. There is nothing new under the sun. All we have to do to find answers is to seek God and study His word, and we will find answers to every question and problem that exist in our lives.

No one on this earth has a perfect life, because no one on this earth is perfect. But I read in the book of Isaiah 26:3 that God said He will keep us in perfect peace, those who keep their minds and heart stayed on Him; for He is our everlasting strength. Desolation, confusion, and trouble may not stop, but we will have God's peace all around us. Now that's the God I serve! Who wouldn't want to serve a God like that? Jesus is the answer to all of our questions and the Savior of us all. We just have to seek Him first.

Today I hear stories of women being abused the same as I was abused. I had no knowledge of shelters for battered women when I was fourteen years of age. Women were beaten by their husbands and boyfriends on a daily basis and received no help from the law or the government, because women were not seeking help. It was just something that was happening to them and they endured.

I thank God that things weren't a lot worse for me, and because of him sending angels to watch over me and my children, we were not consumed. I read somewhere that to err is human, but to forgive is divine. My desire is to do the things that please God, and to live a life of peace for the rest of my life.

I feel extremely blessed today as I write my story. I am also amazed at the life that I had and am still living. I often think that as big as this world is, and considering the billions of people who live on this earth, we can only count those we can truly call a friend on one hand. Some would still have a finger or two left. We have associates and acquaintances who come in and out of our lives, but to call someone friend is another story.

Since we can't control everything that happens to us in this life, and knowing that our dependence is on God, I feel that everyone who comes into our lives are destined to be. I don't believe that meeting these individuals is by happenstance. Whether they come into our lives to harm or to enlighten, I believe there is something we are supposed to learn.

That is why I feel so blessed to be able to say, I do have friends.

To name a few, I will start with Joyce. When I met her for the first time, her name was Joyce Henson. She is now Joyce Cooke. Joyce and I go back a long way. I met her on the job when we worked for the Department of Human Resources. We hit it off in a short time. We were inseparable. We dated two first cousins who had an apartment together. We got to know each other very well, and we raised our children together. I love her children and she loves mine. We met in the early seventies and we remain friends today. Joyce knows things about me, and I know things about her that we will take to the grave, and I am confident that it will stay that way. That is why we call each other friend.

I also have a friend named Brenda Crawford. Brenda and I became friends in the early sixties when we met on the job, working in a department store in northeast Washington.

We remain friends today. Brenda and I would put our money together every month to buy food. We would buy a case of chickens, fifty pounds of potatoes, pounds of dry beans, and flour. We were able to feed our children well. We found that it made a lot of sense, and our children were fed very well and were healthy.

I also met Sherman Keith on the job when I worked for the Federal Protective Service. Keith, as we lovingly call him, was a very friendly person who everyone liked. We liked each other immediately, and we have much respect for each other. I later met his wife, Gloria, and his children. Today we are still very close friends.

A few years later, I met a young lady named Brenda Henderson. My son Floyd introduced us. They met while working at the Pentagon. I will never forget how friendly Brenda was when we met. We stayed in touch down through the years, and she has never changed. Brenda is friendly to everyone she meets. She has a large heart and will do anything for you that is within her power to do. When Brenda learned that I celebrated my birthday on February 2nd, and her birthday was February 3rd, she said that she knew we would get along and always remain friends. I agreed. We understood each other.

I thank God for sending these friends into my life. They have made my life so much richer. Several people have come in and out of my life, and I thank God for them all. I have always gotten something out of the relationships, whether they were positive or negative ones.

As I look back over my life, I realize that God has never left my side. He has always been there to show me something tangible that I could use to grow and prosper. I wasn't certain if my brother Leroy was speaking sarcastically when he said one day, "God sure knew what He was doing when He gave you sons."

Well, even if it was said in a sarcastic way, he was right. God surely knew what He was doing. God always knows what He is doing. He had a plan for me and made me the person that I am today. I am so grateful, and I feel so blessed. He gave me a life that I would never want to trade for all of the money in the world. He not only blessed me with three wonderful sons, He also blessed me with a beautiful, kind, loving daughter, and from them I have been blessed with seven grandchildren and eight great-grandchildren.

I thank God every day for His blessings. Writing this book was therapeutic for me. It helped me to cherish things that happened in my life that I never would have before. It helped me to understand why I did many of the things that I did and why I made the choices I made. Those actions helped me to grow into the woman I am today.

I feel love and compassion for others. I love to serve and give all that I can to make others happy. I am a child of the King and one day I want to hear God say, "Well done, welcome my good and faithful servant. You have been faithful over a few things, so I will make you ruler over many."

I know if I keep my mind on Jesus, the best is yet to come. He promised that if I commit my ways to Him and trust in Him, He shall bring forth my righteousness as the light, and my justice as the noonday. When I think of the goodness of Jesus and all that He has done for me, my soul cries, "Hallelujah, thank You dear God for saving a wretch like me! I once was lost, but now am found. Thank You, dear Lord Jesus, my Savior, for Your amazing grace! Amen."

P.S.

I began writing this book at the age of sixty-nine. I am not sure when this book will be published, but I have faith that one day God will make a way for me to get this book published, but only if it is His will. I am now seventy-four years old, and at the age of seventy I had to come back and revisit my book because I had to tell you how the celebration of our brother Milford went.

I thank God so much for blessing us and always giving us wonderful weather. Although it was a bit windy, we had a good time. It went even better than I imagined it would. Milford was so pleased. He had a special glow on his face when each of us stood and spoke wonderful, encouraging words about him. He was able to see and hear and feel the love that everyone had for him.

Even though it was a day of celebrating him, he still went around and passed out hundred-dollar bills to each of us, his siblings. He is one of a kind, and we love and appreciate him and his kindness toward us. That's just the kind of guy he is and we love him!

I often wear the T-shirt that we all wore the day of his celebration to my exercise class. His face is on the front. One day a lady came up to me and asked, "Who is this gentleman you have on the front of your shirt?"

I replied, "It's my brother."

She got this sad look on her face and said, "Oh, I'm so sorry. When did he pass?"

I said, "He has not passed anywhere, my sister. He is very much alive. I wear this shirt for inspiration to keep me moving with the rest of you."

We both laughed out loud!

I told my brother about it and we both laughed. Since then, we have celebrated another one of our brothers, Lincoln. We will continue to celebrate a sibling once a year. Thank You, dear God, that we can all laugh and count the blessings You continue to surround us with. Angels are still watching over us.

My son Juan was recently diagnosed with prostate cancer. I went to God in prayer and asked Him to heal my son's body. After I prayed, a calmness came over me, and I knew then that God heard my prayers. I want to let you know, because of prayers and trusting in our Lord and Savior, Jesus the Christ, He received favorable results from his treatments and is doing just fine.

A week later, after I received his good news, I received a call from my other son Gregg telling me that he found out from one of his friends that he may be eligible to apply to go back to college and get his master's degree. He thought that his eligibility had run out. After serving twenty years in the army, he went to college and received his bachelor's degree a few years ago. He made some phone calls and found that he was eligible for twelve months and two days of going back to school, and would be paid handsomely to do so. It looks as though I will be going back to

South Carolina to another graduation. God is so good, and I pray that I will be around to do just that!

I will forever praise God for His goodness and tender mercies for blessing our family, and others for sharing the Good News that should be shared all over the world—that God is great and greatly to be praised. Thank You, our Creator and master of the world, our Lord and Savior, Jesus the Christ.

To be continued!!!!

"Amazing grace, how sweet the sound; that saved a wretch like me. I <u>once was lost</u> but now am found, was blind but now I see!"

Written by:

Author, John Newton

Former slave trader

About the Author

MARY EVELYN WASHINGTON BROWN WAS born and raised in Calvert County, Maryland. She is the daughter of the late George Samuel and Annie Rebecca Washington. She moved to Washington, DC, in 1966 to live permanently. She is the ninth child born in a family of thirteen. She had eight brothers and four sisters. As of this date, two brothers and two sisters have passed away. As a young girl she was a dreamer, always fantasizing about the places she would go and the things she would do. She was always reading love novels and placing herself in the cities and countries of the places she read about. She would go out in the woods behind her house, find a large shady tree, clean off the ground around it to make it comfortable, and then spend hours reading. As far back as she can remember of the trials and tribulations in her life, she is certain that angels were always watching over her. This book is about the setbacks and sit ups in her life. When she became a teenager, she wasn't afraid to step out and do some of the things she often dreamed of doing, such as singing in clubs, appearing on television, and traveling. She was able to do most of these. She had the opportunity to travel to one of the places that she read about, the French Quarter in New Orleans, Louisiana. It was a little disappointing because it didn't have the romantic scenery that she read about in books, but the beignets were delicious.